No. ______

In the Supreme Court of the United States

♦

Samuel H. Sloan,
Administrator of Estate
of K. Michael Goodall
with Will Annexed

vs.

Bank of America N. A.

and

Guide Dogs For the Blind, Inc.

♦

On Petition for a Writ of Certiorari to the California Court of Appeal, First Appellate District, Division Four

♦

PETITION FOR A WRIT OF CERTIORARI

♦

Samuel H. Sloan
Administrator of Estate
of K. Michael Goodall
with Will Annexed
461 Peachstone Terrace
San Rafael CA 94903
(415) 419-5980
917-659-3397
samhsloan@gmail.com

Questions Presented

Were the actions or lack thereof by the Judge of the Superior Court of the State of California in which he issued an abrupt ruling without any of the normal procedures, without any discovery being allowed, with no production of documents, no motion for summary judgment filed, no findings of fact and conclusions of law, no fact hearing of any kind, no declarations or statement of facts under oath and none of the recognized procedures for the conduct of any case having been followed constitute such as vast deviation of established legal practice as to constitute a violation of Constitutional Rights to Due Process of Law as guaranteed by the Fifth and Fourteenth Amendments to the Constitution of the United States?

Does the filing of a timely petition for rehearing after the superior court judge abruptly decided this case without any hearing at all toll the time to file a notice of appeal until after the judge has signed the order denying the rehearing?

Did the actions of the superior Court judge in waiting two full months after the had denied the petition for rehearing from the bench but before he signed the order denying rehearing so as to deliberately put the case past the time to file a notice of appeal deprive the estate of the deceased and the heirs of the estate of due the constitutional right to process of law?

Did the actions of the San Francisco Superior Court judge in effectively taking this case away from the Marin County Probate Court which had appointed petitioner as administrator of the estate including the property which is located in Marin County violate the standard rule that all cases jurisdiction involving proceedings concerning real property must take place in the jurisdiction where the property was located which is Marin County?

When a petition in probate has been filed and has been granted by a superior court of a county, may a party be allowed to file a proceeding in some other county where none of the deceased ever lived in that other county, none of their property has ever been located in that other county, where the wills the deceased are all in probate in the first county and there is no connection with the second county of anything having anything to do with this case?

Table of Contents

Exhibit E

Register of Actions in Marin County Probate Court in Estate of K. Michael Goodall, Case No. 1100596

Exhibit F

Register of Actions in Marin County Superior Court Unlawful Detainer Proceedings Case Numbers Civ 1203665 and Civ 1204541 and Order of Dismissal

Exhibit G

Marin County Superior Court Unlawful Detainer Proceedings Case Numbers Civ 1204541 tentative ruling adopted as final ruling denying motion for summary judgment

Exhibit H

San Francisco Probate Court Transcript of Hearing dated July 19, 2012 In Re The Goodall Trust

Exhibit I

San Francisco Probate Court Transcript of Hearing dated September 20, 2012 In Re The Goodall Trust

Exhibit J

San Francisco Probate Court Transcript of Hearing dated October 29, 2012 In Re The Goodall Trust

Exhibit K

San Francisco Probate Court Transcript of Hearing dated November 15, 2012 In Re The Goodall Trust

Exhibit L

Marin County Superior Court Transcript of Hearing dated November 28, 2012 in Bank of America vs. Samuel H. Sloan, et al Case No. CIV 1204541

Exhibit M

Order of Marin County Probate Court Appointing Samuel H. Sloan as Administrator of the Estate of K. Michael Goodall with Will Annexed

Exhibit N

Second Amendment of the Goodall Trust intending to make K. Michael Goodall Trustee of the Trust of September 12, 1990 dated January 19, 1999

Exhibit O

The Goodall Trust dated September 12, 1990

Exhibit P

Purported Last Will of Kenneth F. Goodall

Exhibit Q

Purported Last Will of Rachel Goodall

Exhibit R

Power of Attorney by Rachel Goodall given to Michael Goodall endorsed by Col. Kenneth Goodall

Exhibit S

Declaration filed by James R. Hastings in San Francisco Probate Court stating among other things that he is the attorney for all parties on both sides of this case and that he was the Trust Administration Attorney for the Trust Department of the Bank of America who prepared and witnessed and notarized the documents in this case.

Exhibit T

Purported Signatures of the Kenneth and Rachel Goodall from the FAX produced by Bank of America on top compared with known actual signatures of Kenneth and Rachel Goodall on bottom from the same date. Note that in the real signatures Kenneth and Rachel Goodall used a light blue pen but the FAX supposedly from the same time and date is in heavy black ink.

Exhibit U

Blowups of the Letters FG from the known signatures of Kenneth F. Goodall compared with the purported signature from the FAX. In the known signatures of Kenneth Goodall he signs the FG together with one stroke of the pen. However, in the trust document the top of the F is a different stroke right to left.

Exhibit V

Declaration by Forensic Document Examiner David S. Moore stating that there are significant differences between the known signatures of Kenneth and Rachel Goodall and the signatures on the 1994 Trust such that he cannot determine if the signatures are real or forgeries without seeing the originals.

Exhibit W

Declaration by Susan D. Scribner for Bank of America as Trustee in Opposition to petition Re Determination of the Particular Action does not constitute a contest dated February 2, 2000.

Exhibit X

Points and Authorities by James R. Hastings, Attorney for Bank of America, in Opposition to petition Re Determination of the Particular Action does not constitute a contest dated February 2, 2000.

Exhibit Y

Proof of Service of Points and Authorities in Opposition to petition Re Determination of the Particular Action does not constitute a contest and Declaration by Susan D. Scribner for Bank of America as Trustee in Opposition to petition Re Determination of the Particular Action does not constitute a contest.

Exhibit Z

Blank signature pages of the unsigned 1994 purported trust

Exhibit AA

Declaration by Nancy Rodgers, a neighbor and best friend of Rachel Goodall, stating that what purports to be her signature as a witness to the wills is not her signature and she never signed any such wills, although she did sign a health care directive by Rachel Goodall (stating not to use artificial means to prolong life).

Petition for a Writ of Certiorari

Petitioner Respectfully Prays that a Writ of Certiorari issue to the California Court of Appeal, First Appellate District, Division Four to review the decision of the California Court of Appeal dismissing this appeal on on January 15, 2013. Petition for Rehearing was denied on February 6, 2013. Case No. A137189. The California Supreme Court denied the Petition for Review on April 17, 2013. Case No. S208891

Parties to the Case

Bank of America N. A.
represented by
Gary D. Rothstein
Manatt, Phelps & Phillips, LLP
One Embarcadero Center, 30th Floor
San Francisco CA 94111

Guide Dogs for the Blind
represented by
Alicia A. Adornato
Attorney for Guide Dogs for the Blind
Reed Smith LLP
101 Second Street, Suite 1800
San Francisco CA 94105

James R. Hastings
1003 3rd Street
San Rafael, CA 94901
represented by
Don A. Lesser
1010 B Street
Suite 350
San Rafael CA 94901

Please note: Although Don Lesser states that he no longer represents James R. Hastings, he appeared in this case and has never filed a notice of withdrawal from this case.

Constitutional Provisions Involved

The Fifth Amendment to the United States Constitution provides:

[N]or shall any person . . . be deprived of life, liberty, or property, without due process of law . . . .

Section One of the Fourteenth Amendment to the United States Constitution provides:

[N]or shall any State deprive any person of life, liberty, or property, without due process of law . . . .

Table of Cases

There are no cases involved in this case. In none of the pleadings filed by Bank of America have they ever cited a case or any legal authority supporting what they have done in this case, which is filing a petition in a different county from where probate is pending, from where all the property is located, from where all the decedents died and are buried, from where all their documents were executed and from where all of their wills are lodged.

OPINIONS BELOW

There are no opinions below. Neither the San Francisco Superior Court, nor the California Court of Appeal, First Appellate District, Division Four nor the California Supreme Court has issued any written or oral decision in this case.

Jurisdiction

The California Court of Appeal, First Appellate District, Division Four, dismissed this appeal on on January 15, 2013 with a summary order stating:

"Appellant Samuel Sloan purports to appeal from an order that was issued by the San Francisco Superior Court concerning a trust. The order at issue was filed on May 16, 2012, therefore appellant had no more than 180 days from that date to file his notice of appeal. (See Cal. Rules of Court, rule 8.104(a)(1)(C).) Appellant's notice of appeal, filed on November 21, 2012, is too late. Dismissal is mandatory. (See rule 8.104(b).) The appeal is dismissed."

Petition for Rehearing was denied on February 6, 2013. Case No. A137189.

The California Supreme Court denied the Petition for Review on April 17, 2013. Case No. S208891

However, the judge of the San Francisco Superior Court had waited two full months before signing the order submitted to him. The order was submitted to the judge for signing on July 27, 2012. The judge did not sign it until September 26, 2012 and it was entered the following day. This had put it beyond the appeal time. Case No. PTR-99-273030

http://webaccess.sftc.org/Scripts/Magic94/mgrqispi94.dll?APPNAME=IJS&PRGNAME=ROA22&ARGUMENTS=-APTR99273030

The parallel case in Marin County is Case No. PRO1100596

Statement of the Case

This case is running in parallel between two different courts in Marin and San Francisco, with opposite results. In the San Francisco case, the case is Case No. PTR 99-273030. In Marin County, the Case numbers are PRO1100596 and CV1204541.

In almost every instance, the issues in the San Francisco Case are exactly the same as the issues in the Marin Case, yet the results have been the opposite. For example, the Bank of America filed a Statute of Limitations Claim in the Marin case. Judge Verna Adams dismissed that claim in a reasoned and lengthy opinion on April 16, 2012. Undaunted, Bank of America filed exactly the same claim in San Francisco, which resulted in an order from which an appeal is taken here.

Similarly, The Bank of America took the ruling by the San Francisco Court here and tried to enforce it over in Marin in a motion for summary judgment. However, the Marin County Superior Court Judge denied the claim by Bank of America, saying that the San Francisco order was interlocutory and non-final and thus non-enforcable in Marin. The Marin County judge ruled that Bank of America must file a claim to quiet title in Marin since the property is in Marin. However, throughout the more than two years that this litigation has been going on, Bank of America has been unwilling to submit its claims to the jurisdiction of the Marin courts, for reasons best known to Bank of America. This has resulted in this stalemate which will take action by the appellate courts to resolve.

Because of these conflicting decisions by different judges in different courts, the situation is in stalemate. The Goodall Estate consists of an estimated two million

dollars in cash and securities plus a house known as "The Goodall Mansion" located at 461 Peachstone Terrace, San Rafael California 94903. Bank of America has the money, having stolen it back in 1999 which resulted in this case, PTR 99-273030, whereas the Estate of Goodall has possession and control of the house. Bank of America has been unsuccessful thus far in its efforts to oust the Goodall Estate from the house.

There is nothing going on in the Superior Court Cases in either Marin or San Francisco at the present time. Thus, it appears that unless this court reviews this case, the parties will be locked in stalemate for an extended period of time, possibly even for years or forever.

On January 15, 2013, The California Court of Appeal dismissed summarily the appeal in this complicated case without waiting for the normal record, briefs and argument. Petitioner therefore did not get a chance to present his case to this court.

K. Michael Goodall died on October 5, 2010 in his home known as "The Goodall Mansion" at 461 Peachstone Terrace in San Rafael, Marin County, California. Petitioner found the Goodall Will among his papers and filed it in Marin County Probate Court on January 28, 2011. On February 1, 2011, Petitioner filed a petition in probate. After consents were obtained from all of the heirs of the Goodall Estate, petitioner petitioned and after two hearings was appointed administrator of the estate.

Petitioner had the key to the house, as he has been a resident of the house. However, on February 28, 2011, while petitioner was away for a few days, there was a break-in and burglary in the house. The entire contents of the house was removed including all legal papers and documents of the Goodalls. When the burglary was discovered, 911 was called and this was reported as a burglary. Deputy Anthony Savas of the Marin County Sheriff's Department responded to the call. Deputy Savas said that he had been patrolling the area during the previous days and had observed a large trash dumpster in front of the house with a Spanish guy bringing stuff out of the house and putting it in the dumpster. However, Deputy Savas had not stopped to inquire, as this had seemed to be a routine case of somebody moving out.

After discovering that the Goodall Mansion had been burgled, the contents removed and the locks on the doors changed, Petitioner as well as heirs of the Goodall Estate searched for several weeks for the stolen Goodall stuff. Finally, by chance it was located in an Auction House in Alameda. The auction House identified Hamilton Kipp as the person who had brought the Goodall Estate stuff to the auction house. It was later established that Hamilton Kipp is an employee of Bank of America. Hamilton Kipp in turn had been told to break into the house and take all the stuff by James R. Hastings, a Marin County Estate

Planning Attorney.

Petitioner filed an 850 Motion in Marin County Probate Court to recover estate property, namely the Goodall Stuff that had been taken by Hamilton Kipp. After two hearings before the Marin County Probate Judge, in June, 2011, Bank of America was forced to return the Goodall Stuff.

However, in the meantime, on April 21, 2011, Bank of America by way of collateral attack had filed a petition in San Francisco Superior Court seeking essentially to overturn the Marin County Probate Order which had listed among other things the Goodall Mansion as an asset of the Goodall Estate. In filing this new petition, Bank of America had used an old case number, PTR 99-273030. That was the number of a case Michael Goodall had filed in December 21, 1999 shortly after his mother had died in which he has sought the removal of Bank of America as Trustee on many grounds including the grounds that Bank of America was not the bank named in the Trust documents and that the proper trustee was Michael Goodall himself and if not himself then at least some bank not openly hostile to him as Bank of America was.

That 1999 case had never been finally decided because after a hearing Mike Goodall had run out of money to the fight the case and because Bank of America was using the funds in the Goodall Estate to fight him. The attorneys for Bank of America told him that if he did not stop fighting the case then the entire estate would be exhausted in attorneys fees and he would be left with nothing.

The attorneys for Bank of America have also been making the same statement in the current branch of the case, but this threat is less effective now because the Attorneys for Bank of America can and perhaps already have striped away all of the assets of the Goodall Estate, so there will be nothing left for the heirs anyway.

An attorney for Bank of America has informed one of the Goodall Heirs there is no money left in the estate. However, when Rachel Goodall died in June 1999 there was approximately one million dollars in the Goodall Estate plus the Goodall Mansion was worth an estimated $700,000. So, if truly the money is entirely gone that means that Bank of America has consumed the entire one million dollars in administration and attorneys fees. However, they must keep fighting this case because if they lose this appeal they will have to pay back the entire one million, plus interest.

The Living Trust set up by Kenneth and Rachel Goodall back in 1990 makes Michael Goodall the beneficiary of the trust. He also becomes the successor trustee of the trust if one or both of his parents dies. The only way a bank becomes a trustee is if Mike is declared incompetent by a court of competent jurisdiction. No such thing has happened.

The 1990 Trust names Security Pacific Bank as the Trustee. In a hearing on November 28, 2012 in Marin Superior Court, counsel for Bank of America said that Bank of America had become Trustee because:

> First, Security Specific Bank became Bank of America back in 1991. We were the successor. You'll probably take judicial notice of it, but that was a very big transaction.

See Transcript of the hearing of November 28, 2012 page 13 which is part of the record of this appeal.

However, this is not what happened. What happened was in 1992 Bank of America NT&SA purchased the assets of Security Pacific Bank. Then in 1998 Nations Bank in North Carolina purchased the assets of Bank of America NT&SA. Subsequently Nations Bank changed its name to Bank of America Corporation, which is a bank holding company located in Charlotte, North Carolina. Thus, the Bank of America today is a completely different entity from either Security Pacific Bank or Bank of America NT&SA.

Counsel for Bank of America must be claiming that the two purchases of the assets of another bank in the 1992 and 1998 transactions also included the purchase of the "right" to be the Successor Trustee to the Goodall Trust. It will take a review of the documents involved in these corporate transactions to determine if the purchase of the assets includes the purchase of the right to be the successor trustee. However, none of this is of any moment because the January 1999 Amendment to the Goodall Trust, namely the Second Amendment to the Goodall Trust, makes Mike Goodall the co-trustee along with his mother. Thus, when Rachel Goodall died in June 1999 Michael Goodall survived as the sole trustee and Bank of America never became the legal trustee.

Bank of America knows this because an attorney for Bank of America drafted the Second Amendment to the Goodall trust.

Page 18 of a trust document, which Bank of America claims is controlling, but which we are prepared to prove was never signed by any of the Goodalls, contains the following provision:

> "(d) If MICHAEL does not survive the surviving settler and leaves no issue who survive the surviving settler, the trustee shall distribute the trust property twenty thousand dollars ($20,000) to each of the then living brothers and sisters of the trustor RACHEL A. Goodall and the remainder to GUIDE DOGS OF MARIN , INC. of San Rafael California."

The problem is that this provision only applies if Michael dies BEFORE his parents do. However, Mike survived his parents by 11 years. Kenneth F. Goodall was born 01 Mar 1916 and died 10 Sep 1994 at age 78. His Social Security Number was 444-40-8884. Rachel A. Goodall was born 23 May 1916 and died 07 Jun 1999. Her Social Security Number was 359-07-1738. Kenneth Michael Goodall was born 13 Jan 1946 and died 05 Oct 2010. His Social Security Number was 559-70-3352.

Since Mike Goodall died 11 years after his parents did, that paragraph does not apply. More than that, nowhere in the entire documents, nearly 40 pages long, is there any mention of what happens if Mike dies after his parents do, except that the trust documents state that the trust is "dissolved" after the death of Mike Goodall.

This provision and the entire document makes it completely 100% clear that the Goodall Estate belongs entirely to Mike Goodall and his heirs, unless Mike Goodall dies before his parents do. There is no possible way that Guide Dogs for the Blind gets anything out of the Goodall Estate. Under no interpretation of the Goodall Trust does Guide Dogs for the Blind get anything.

Yet, Bank of America, in its initial petition filed in San Francisco Superior Court, said that it was due to drafting errors that the trust documents mistakenly do not give any money to Guide Dogs for the Blind. Bank of America asked the Superior Court to in effect rewrite the trust documents so as to give the Goodall Estate to the Dogs.

At the first hearing in San Francisco Superior Court on May 25, 2011, Petitioner appeared in pro per because he felt it absurd and ridiculous that Bank of America would file their petition, because the trust documents clearly DO NOT give any part of the Goodall Estate to the Dogs and secondly because this case was already pending as a probate case in Marin County that clearly had jurisdiction. The Goodalls all lived and died in Marin County, all of their property including their house was in Marin County, all their documents were executed in Marin County and there was nothing about this case that had anything to do with San Francisco County. Thus, San Francisco County obviously does not have jurisdiction. Petitioner expected that the San Francisco Court would throw the case out immediately.

In addition, Guide Dogs for the Blind is behind all of the other heirs. The trust provides that each of the Goodall siblings gets $20,000. Rachel Goodall had five siblings, three brothers and two sisters, and Kenneth Goodall had two brothers. Many of them are dead but they all married and had children, some of whom were adopted. There are about twenty Goodall heirs listed on the service list and they all have the right to contest this case. Clearly, only the Marin County Probate Court has the jurisdiction, venue and competence to decide these claims.

In addition, the direct heirs of Michael Goodall may have a claim. The trust provides that his wife and/or children inherit from the trust.

Guide Dogs for the Blind are at the bottom of the totem pole. This case goes to the dogs and they get money only after all these other people and even then the Dogs do not get anything unless Michael dies before either of his parents do, which did not happen.

Because of all these factors, Petitioner did not take seriously the petition filed by Bank of America in San Francisco. Petitioner assumed that the San Francisco case would either be dismissed or else transferred to the right court, which was Marin County Probate Court.

Petitioner was thus shocked when the San Francisco judge with a wave of the hand and without giving any reason for the decision or indeed without saying anything at all ruled in favor of Bank of America and signed an order that had been handed up without even allowing the Petitioner to see and comment on the order that was being signed.

Petitioner then realized that he had better retain counsel. After a long search, Petitioner found a qualified attorney willing to represent the Goodall Estate on a Contingency Fee basis. This was necessary because Bank of America had already taken all the money. The Goodalls had never had an account with Bank of America, not even a simple checking account. Col. Goodall was retired military officer, so most of the Goodall money was with USAA Investment Management in San Antonio, Texas. There were also smaller amounts with mutual finds and stock trading accounts. None of this was with Bank of America or anywhere in the state of California.

Right after Rachel Goodall had died in June 1999, Bank of America through its attorney James R. Hastings had contacted USAA Investment Management and directed that all Goodall funds be transferred to Bank of America. Michael Goodall had not been told about this and had no idea that this had happened. In short order, all of the bank accounts that Mike Goodall had been operating were stripped of their assets. Mike Goodall was left destitute and without funds. That is the reason why he filed this case on December 21, 1999.

Bank of America completely stonewalled, as they continue to do this day. They refused and still continue to refuse to give Mike Goodall or indeed any of the Goodalls any information about what happened to the Goodall Millions. It was as if the funds had disappeared into a Black Hole.

After the adverse ruling on May 25, 2011, Petitioner was able to retain counsel in time for the next hearing in San Francisco Probate Court. Meanwhile, several hearings on the same subject matter had been held in Marin County Probate

Court.

It is important at all times to remember that this case is running in parallel in two different courts: San Francisco Superior Court and Marin County Probate Court. Obviously, the Marin County Court is the right court and at each hearing in San Francisco Petitioner has demanded transfer of this case to Marin.

At the next hearing in San Francisco, Bank of America brought attorney James R. Hastings to court prepared to have him testify as a witness as he had been attorney for all parties including the Goodalls, the Goodall Trust and the Bank of America. Hastings was going to testify that the money should go to the Dogs. This was one of just many obvious conflicts on interest by James R. Hastings. However, Petitioner's new counsel Sam Ware asked for the opportunity of discovery. Bank of America protested vehemently and said that there should be no discovery at all. They especially objected to any discovery of the money. They refused to reveal anything about the Goodall millions, about how much it was, were they had gotten it from and what they had done with it.

Finally, Judge Mary Wiss agreed that there should be discovery. Whereas Bank of America wanted to hold a hearing and finish the case that day, the superior court judge said that there should be discovery.

However, as will be seen there has never been any discovery on this case, because Bank of America has been completely stonewalling. Not even one document has been produced either by Bank of America or attorney James R. Hastings. Bank of America has absolutely refused to produce anything. They even refuse to produce the Goodall Trust upon which their claims are based. James R. Hastings has testified that he has lost the files and thus does not have anything. In addition he has stated that to provide any discovery would violate the attorney Client Privilege of Bank of America because he was counsel for Bank of America at the same time that he was counsel for the Goodalls.

Sam Ware then subpoenaed James R. Hastings for a deposition and required him to bring all documents and files pertaining to this case. Hastings appeared for the deposition on November 14, 2011 but did not bring any documents at all. His attorney Don Lesser said that the subpoena was overbroad and as Hastings had been attorney for Bank of America too it would violate the attorney client privilege of Bank of America and that the files and notes pertaining to this case had all been lost. At the oral deposition, Hastings testified that basically he could not remember anything about the case.

On December 14, 2011 Sam Ware filed a motion for discovery and production of documents pertaining to this case.

On December 29, 2011, Don A. Lesser, Counsel for James Hastings, filed opposition to the motions for discovery, saying that it would be "oppressive and burdensome" upon James R. Hastings and also violate the attorney client privilege of Bank of America because James R. Hastings had been attorney for Bank of America at the same time that he was attorney for the Goodall and the Goodall Trust.

Not long thereafter Don Lesser withdrew as counsel for James R. Hastings.

On January 20, 2012, Judge Busch denied the motion for production of documents, especially the trust Document, but said that James R. Hastings was required to search his files to look for the trust and if he could find it he was required to produce it and otherwise he must file a declaration stating what efforts he had made to find the trust.

On February 2, 2012, James R. Hastings filed a declaration stating that he had searched all his files and was unable to find the Goodall Trust.

On February 6, 2012, Nancy Rodgers, a friend and neighbor of the Goodalls, filed a declaration stating that her purported signatures on the Goodall Wills, which were pour over wills pouring money into the trust, were not her signatures and she had never signed such a document. As there had never been any money in the trust, these pour over wills were essential to the claims by Bank of America and Guide Dogs for the Blind to be entitled to any of the Goodall millions.

After several more pleadings were filed on all sides, on April 24, 2012, Bank of America filed an additional reply asserting for the first time in this case that objections to the 1994 Trust were time-barred by a Statute of Limitations. Although this was the first time Bank of America had made this claim in this case, they had made exactly the same claim in the parallel proceeding going on in Marin County Probate Court. That claim had been dismissed by Marin County Probate Judge Verna Adams in a lengthy and reasoned decision on April 16, 2012. The statute of limitations claim was also entirely bogus for several reasons the most obvious being that Michael Goodall had indeed contested the right of Bank of America to be the trustee by filing this very case on December 21, 1999. Also, the statute of limitations claim was not accompanied by any evidence or a declaration in support. In addition, the words "as amended" had been omitted or when it was included, obviously it logically referred to the 1999 Amendment to the Trust which had made Mike Goodall the Trustee. The 1990 Trust had made Michael Goodall the beneficiary of the trust and the 1999 Amendment had made Michael the co-trustee of the trust, so there was no reason for Michael to object to either of them.

Because of the shortness of time before the previously scheduled hearing, Samuel Sloan and his counsel did not have time to respond to this "additional reply" and so asked for additional time which was denied from the bench. And so, Judge Busch signed the order dated May 16, 2012 from which the first appeal is taken, without a fact hearing of any kind and without any findings of fact or conclusions of law.

On May 25, 2012, seven days after the entry of the order of May 16, 2012, Samuel Sloan filed through counsel a motion for discovery to compel the production of documents including the documents forming the basis of the newly made statute of limitations claim. This was not filed as a motion for reconsideration, because Sloan through counsel deemed the May 16, 2012 order to be an interlocutory order, not a final judgment, because, among many other things it does not use the word "judgment", and does not dispose of all of the issues involved in this case. However, this motion was filed within the time limit for motions for reconsideration to be on the safe side in case the courts were later to decide that it was a judgment.

Sam Sloan, Administrator of the Goodall Estate, had been caught off guard by the May 16, 2012 decision because he had naturally assumed that there would be some sort of trial or fact hearing and Bank of America would be required to present their evidence if any before the court would rule. It was not to be expected that the judge would decide this complicated case abruptly from the bench without any hearing. Because of this surprise ruling, the administrator started searching through the 40 or 50 storage boxes of material Bank of America had stolen when they broke into the Goodall Mansion on February 28, 2011 but then were forced to return on June 10, 2011 by proceedings in the Marin County Probate Court.

During these searches, the administrator found a treasure trove of documents. All or almost all of these documents had been prepared by James R. Hastings, Attorney for Bank of America, so Bank of America had these documents all along but had failed to produce them. Of great importance was a Power of Attorney the Goodall Parents, Kenneth and Rachel Goodall, had given their son Michael on August 24, 1994 on the Death Bed of Kenneth, placing Michael with power of attorney over the Goodall Trust. This proved that the claim by the Attorney of Bank of America that the Goodall parents did not trust Michael with their money was false. Also included in the same treasure trove of documents was a signed health care directive by Kenneth Goodall that he be allowed to die of the Esophageal cancer of which he was suffering at the time and an unsigned 1994 Goodall Trust showing that Kenneth had never signed the 1994 amendment to the trust. Kenneth Goodall was in the final stages of cancer and a feeding tube had been inserted in his abdomen on July 17, 1994. He died on September 10, 1994. These documents were included in the exhibits Sloan filed in his May 25, 2012 motion.

On the same date, Sloan filed a declaration of David S. Moore, a highly regarded forensic document examiner, who stated that upon comparing the known and authentic signatures of Kenneth Goodall found on other documents, on checks, on his personal notebook and the like and comparing them with the signature on the purported 1994 amendment to the trust, they were not consistent but he could not made a final determination as to whether the signature was authentic or not without being allowed to examine the actual Goodall Trust document, but such an examination had been denied.

On June 27, 2012, Gary Rothstein, attorney for Bank of America served on Sam Sloan and his counsel Sam Ware a motion for sanctions against the Motion for Discovery dated May 25, 2012 asking for sanctions against Sam Sloan personally and against Sam Ware personally in the amount of $16,000 for filing the motion for discovery which they deemed to be a motion for reconsideration. In a cover letter, Gary Rothstein, attorney for Bank of America, stated that unless the motion for reconsideration were withdrawn he would file the motion for sanctions, effectively blackmailing the Goodall Estate.

It is important to remember here that Sloan is a volunteer administrator of the trust because the Goodall Trust has no money because Bank of America stole it all and Sloan is not named in the will. In addition, Attorney Sam Ware took this case as a contingency case. By serving this motion for sanctions Bank of America was threatening Sloan and his counsel with a substantial financial loss whereas they had nothing to gain from this case.

So, the Administrator of the Goodall estate had everything to lose and nothing to gain by continuing this case.

On June 29, 2012 Guide Dogs for the Blind joined this motion by filing their own motion for sanctions for filing this petition for rehearing.

Nevertheless, the administrator and his counsel did not Cave.

A hearing was held on these motions on July 19, 2012. Judge Busch denied the motion which he deemed to be a motion for reconsideration and he also denied the motion by Bank of America and Guide Dogs for the Blind for Sanctions against the Administrator of the Goodall Estate and Sam Ware, Counsel for the Goodall Estate.

On July 20, 2012, the very next day, Bank of America filed a new motion for Sanctions against the Administrator of the Goodall Estate and against Sam Ware Counsel for the Goodall Estate seeking sanctions in the amount of between $13,000 and $16,000 against each of them. This motion had been denied from the bench the previous day so obviously nothing had changed.

On July 27, 2012, the parties submitted for the judge's signature an order denying the motion for reconsideration heard on July 19, 2012. Sam Sloan,

Administrator of the Estate, planned and intended to file a notice of appeal as soon as the order was signed. Instead the judge sat on the order for two full months and did not sign in until September 26, 2012. It was entered the following day. This delay of two months put it past the normal time for filing a notice of appeal.

On August 14, 2012, Bank of America filed a third Motion for Sanctions against the Administrator of the Goodall Estate and his attorney.

On September 7, 2012, as a result of having three successive motions for sanctions filed against him, Sam Ware filed a motion to be relieved as counsel. He said that he could not effectively oppose the repeated motions for sanctions against him while also acting as counsel for the estate. No man can serve to masters so he needed to be relieved as counsel so that he could defend himself against actions by Bank of America and their counsel which threatened his professional career.

Now again Sloan could not file his notice of appeal because he had to wait until the judge decided the motion for sanctions and the motion by his counsel to withdraw to escape the sanctions. As Sloan was represented by Counsel he could not file the Notice of Appeal by himself. In addition, as these motions affected the merits of the case and the judge was retaining jurisdiction over the case there remained the possibility that the judge would reverse himself and the case would continue.

Finally, the judge held his hearing on the motion to withdraw which was strenuously opposed by Sloan and granted the motion on November 15, 2012. On the same day, Judge Busch held his hearing on the motion for sanctions and denied that motion, basically saying that there was enough grounds for Counsel for the Goodall Estate to file a motion for reconsideration but not enough grounds for him to grant it.

On September 21, 2012, Judge Busch signed the order denying the Motion for Sanctions. Sloan filed his notice of appeal the very same day.

ARGUMENT

The Court of Appeal dismissed the first appeal as untimely. Petitioner contends that it was not untimely because of the inappropriate and indeed unethical actions of both opposing counsel and the Superior Court judge. Opposing counsel kept filing motions even after the order appealed from. They filed three successive motions for sanctions in the amount of more than $13,000 against Petitioner and his counsel. It is important that Petitioner is a unpaid volunteer administrator because there is no money in the Goodall Estate and trust as Bank of America stole all the money. Petitioner is also not an heir to the Goodall estate. However, the real heirs to the Goodall Estate are depending on Petitioner to win this case because if Bank of America wins the heirs will get nothing zero, as all the money will go to the Dogs.

So, by filing these groundless motions by two of the biggest law firms in San Francisco Petitioners counsel became afraid to file an appeal. In addition, Petitioner could not retain another attorney either as every attorney he consulted was afraid that he too would be on the wrong end of a motion for sanctions by Bank of America.

Next, Petitioner filed a motion for discovery. The superior court had ruled in favor of a new claim by Bank of America that a Statute of Limitations barred petitioner's defense. This claim was obviously bogus because Mike Goodall had filed this very case back in 1999 to object to Bank of America being the trustee.

Thirdly, the judge delayed two months in signing the order. This delay of two months by the judge was what put the case over the time limit to file the appeal.

The order was submitted to the judge for signing on July 27, 2012. The judge did not sign it until September 26, 2012.

Next the order that Judge Busch has not been after proper notice and a hearing. Indeed, there has never been a fact hearing in this case. There has never been sworn testimony of any witnesses. There has been no discovery. No documents have been produced. Hastings says that he has lost the trust documents. If you look at the case files you will see that there have been no declarations, no exhibits, no verifications, no findings of facts and conclusions of law.

Neither Bank of America nor Guide Dogs for the Blind have ever filed a brief or a memorandum of law in this case. They have never cited a case, they have never explained upon what legal grounds or theory of law they are entitled to proceed. They have not even explained what they are even doing appearing in this case as the Goodalls all died more than two years ago. They have no standing to be appearing in this case. Only the contestants, namely Guide Dogs and the legitimate heirs have standing.

Meanwhile, James R. Hastings, who says that he has lost the documents, is teaching a class in Estate Planning. On page 15 of the current Tamalpais Union High School District Summer Camp Sneak Preview there is an ad for the next course by James Hastings. It is called Estate Planning 101. The next class starts on April 23, 2013 and the fee to attend the class is $25.

In The Alternative this Court Should Treat this as a Writ Petition

Petitioner has annexed a verification to satisfy one of the requirements for a writ petition. Under Olson v. Cory (1983) 35 Cal.3d 390, 401 [197 Cal. Rptr. 843, 673 P.2d 720] an appeal can only be considered as a writ petition under entirely unusual circumstances. It is submitted that the unusual circumstances exist here in that this case is running in parallel in two different courts and the courts have ruled in the opposite way. The Marin Courts have ruled in favor of Petitioner whereas the San Francisco court has ruled in favor of Bank of America.

At a hearing in Marin County Superior Court on November 28, 2012 in which Bank of America sought to enforce the order from which this appeal was taken, Judge Roy Chernus ruled that the May 2012 order was not a final judgment and was interlocutory. According to that ruling this appeal is unnecessary. However, Bank of America disagrees. They consider May 2012 the San Francisco order to be the final judgment. As a result this case is stalemated.

Since this court has never seen the record of this appeal because the Superior Court never had time to transmit it, it could not have understood the complex issues in this case. As Judge Roy Chernus of Marin County Superior Court stated in a one of the related cases in Marin County, "this is not your usual garden variety type of action" because while this case has been pending in the San Francisco Probate Court the same case has been pending over in the Marin County Probate Court. Two courts have been handling the same case.

Plaintiff here, Bank of America, lost their initial motions over in Marin County and then opted for the greener pastures in San Francisco Probate Court. As this case has progressed, every time Bank of America lost a motion over in Marin County they filed the same motion in San Francisco where they won.

Regarding the statute of limitations claim that Bank of America made in an "Additional Reply" in which the Administrator of the Goodall Estate did not have a chance to respond, Bank of America had made exactly the same Statute of Limitations claim in Marin County and Judge Verna Adams had dismissed that claim in a reasoned and lengthy opinion on April 16, 2012. Undaunted, Bank of America made that identical claim on San Francisco Probate Court.

Of immediate concern is the court felt that the appeal from the May 16, 2012 was untimely. However, Petitioner contends that this is not correct because Petitioner was prevented by the actions of opposing counsel and actions of the judge which made it impossible for him to file the appeal any sooner than he did. Indeed, Petitioner waited in the court room for the San Francisco Judge to sign his final order in this case so he could go down to the filing room to file this notice of appeal.

In view of the actions of the San Francisco Probate Judge in making this case

"Appeal Proof" by among other things waiting a full two months before signing the order denying the petition for rehearing the judge prevented an earlier appeal. The order was submitted to the judge for signing on July 27, 2012. The judge did not sign it until September 26, 2012.

More than that, actions by Bank of America and Guide Dogs for the Blind unethically made it impossible for Petitioner to retain new counsel. They did this by repeatedly filing motions for sanctions against existing counsel. Their first motion for sanctions which demanded attorneys fees between $13,000 and $16,000 against both the Administrator of the Goodall Estate and his counsel was filed on June 29, 2012. That motion was denied by Judge Busch on June 19, 2012.

However, on the very next day, July 20, 2012, Bank of America filed a second motion for sanctions even though nothing had changed overnight since the first denial.

A Third Motion for Sanctions was filed by Bank of America on August 14, 2012.

All these motions for sanctions filed by a big and powerful Bank of America and their counsel one of the largest law firms in California had the effect of understandably frightening the counsel for the Goodall estate. As no man can serve two masters, he felt that he had to withdraw as counsel for the estate in order to defend himself against these successive motion for sanctions which threatened his professional career.

As a result, Petitioner had no choice but to wait until these motions for sanctions and motion to withdraw were decided before he could file this notice of appeal. Petitioner was literally waiting in the courtroom for the judge to sign these orders so he could run down to the clerks office and file this notice of appeal the same day.

If this court decides that this appeal is untimely in spite of these considerations, Petitioner requests that this appeal be construed as a writ petition. Since Petitioner does not have an appellate remedy since the court took so long to decide the motion, the time to appeal the underlying judgment had expired before he knew the outcome, but had petitioner appealed that judgment earlier, the trial court would then have lost jurisdiction to deal with the matter.

If this court finds the appeal untimely, this court should considering the merits on a writ petition, on the ground that there was no appellate remedy. Petitioner in no way caused this delay.

After considering this matter, this court should dismiss this case entirely. The proper Probate Proceeding involving the Goodall Estate is now pending over in Marin County Probate Court. Case No. PR 1100596. Everything about this case happened over in Marin. The only reason Bank of America filed in San Francisco is they do not like the judge over in Marin.

We believe that the May 16, 2012 order is not a final judgment. It does not contain the word "Judgment". It does not include findings of fact and conclusions of law. It does not award money or property to anybody.

However, the orders of the San Francisco Court cannot be ignored because Bank of America claims that it is a judgment and they have moved to enforce it as a judgment.

In August and October, 2012 Bank of America filed two unlawful detainer actions in Marin County seeking to evict the Goodall heirs from the Goodall Mansion at 461 Peachstone Terrace San Rafael, California. These actions were unsuccessful, for the same reason Petitioner has stated from the beginning. Judge Chernus wrote:

> As against Sam Sloan and Kayo Kimura plaintiff seeks judgment for possession based on orders of the San Francisco Superior Court and the July 27, 2012, Sixty-day notice. Plaintiff has put its title to the property "at issue" in this unlawful detainer proceeding. The bulk of the allegations in the Complaint and the "Undisputed Facts" in support of the subject motion for summary judgment are addressed to plaintiffs extensive efforts by way of collateral proceedings in San Francisco Superior Court to confirm that the premises is an asset of the Trust for Michael created under the Goodall Trust dated September 12,l990, that title to the premises is in Bank America as trustee, and that plaintiff may administer the premises pursuant to the terms of Trust.
>
> Yet despite plaintiffs extensive allegations detailing the San Francisco proceedings, plaintiff does not actually allege or demonstrate via undisputed facts that the orders of the SF Sup. Court are final or that the issue of its title to the subject property has been fully and finally determined.
>
> Plaintiff appears to base its right to commence this unlawful detainer proceeding upon the Minute Order of the SF Superior Court dated July 19, 2012, denying defendant's petition for reconsideration as plaintiff served the subject 60-Day Notice eight days later on July 27,2012, even though the court's order was not formally entered until September 27, 2012. (See Complaint, par. 19, and Exh. E) Even assuming the order denying defendant's petition for reconsideration constitutes a final and binding determination of plaintiffs title (though not specifically alleged) plaintiff served the 60-day notice before that order was formally entered on September 27, 2012. This unlawful detainer action was filed a mere 12-

> days later on October 9, 2012. As stated by the Court in Greenhut v. Wooden {1982} 129 Cal.App.3d 64,68, this is not your usual garden variety type of unlawful detainer action where the issue of title is strictly limited. Having put its own title in issue and by relying on the San Francisco Trust proceeding as the source of its authority to commence this proceeding plaintiff should demonstrate that title to the property has, in fact, been finally adjudicated in its favor. Plaintiff's pleading and evidence falls falls short of demonstrating a final adjudication of title in its favor and raises a question of fact whether the alleged 60-day notice was served prematurely.
>
> As to defendants Hoppe and Thornally, a complaint for unlawful detainer must allege that the tenant continues in possession of the premises. (CCP $1161.) No cause of action for unlawful detainer exists if the tenant has quit before the action is filed. Defendants Hoppe and Thornally have filed answers admitting they have relinquished possession of the premises. In its motion, plaintiff claims that while Hoppe and Thornally have relinquished physical possession of the premises, "plaintiff is informed that Hoppe and Thornally have not relinquished their alleged right to possession of the premises." If a landlord wishes to determine rights to possession but not physical possession, it cannot do so by way of summary unlawful detainer; a quiet title action would be the proper remedy.

Thusly, Judge Chernus stated in essence the same thing petitioner Sloan has been saying from the first pleading which is that the only way for Bank of America to get what it wants is to file an action in Marin County. Bank of America can never succeed in obtaining access to real property in Marin by bringing a case in San Francisco.

This action by Bank of America should be dismissed and thrown out of court for a deeper reason, which is that Bank of America has never had standing in this case. Bank of America was never the legal trustee of the Goodall Trust. Kenneth and Rachel Goodall were the trustees. Upon the death of Kenneth, the Trust documents which are annexed as exhibits show that Michael became the co-trustee with his mother and upon her death Michael became the sole trustee. At no time did Bank of America have any rights in this case. They simply usurped and stole this case because of the millions of dollars involved.

What happened is Bank of America stole the money, pure and simple. They have no right and no claim to the Goodall assets.

In addition, Guide Dogs for the Blind has no standing and no claim. The trust document upon which Bank of America and Guide Dogs for the Blind relies (although they have failed and refused to produce it and claimed to have lost it) does not establish their right.

Paragraph 6, note 1 of the petition filed by Bank of America contains the following noteworthy statement.

"The Provisions of the Bypass Trust are somewhat unclear with respect to the proper beneficiaries of the Trust for Michael in the wake of Mike Goodall's Death."

"Somewhat unclear" is a massive understatement or misstatement. I have shown the trust documents to several attorneys specializing in such matters. All of them say that the trust documents are nonsense. "Absurd", "ridiculous" and several other adjectives are used to describe these trust documents. A well known San Francisco attorney (who I prefer not to name) told me that the attorney who drew up this trust should be disbarred for incompetence.

For all of these reasons this appeal should be reinstated.

Reasons for Granting the Writ

Nowadays it seems that the papers are filled with allegations of misconduct by Bank of America in taking over properties and evicting people from their homes. Those cases usually involve mortgages. However, in this case no mortgage is involved. The Goodalls built their house with their own money and never borrowed from a bank. They never had a bank account with Bank of America, not even a simple checking account. The Goodalls notoriously mistrusted and hated attorneys. None of their documents make any mention of Bank of America even though the drafting attorney, James R. Hastings, was the head of the trust department of the Bank of America at the time.

We can prove that the Goodalls never signed and could not have signed the key document which Bank of America says that Col. Goodall signed because he was hospitalized and on life support at that time and thus could not possibly have gone to the office of James R. Hastings in San Rafael to sign the document. The highly regarded handwriting expert says that the FAXed copies (the only copies Bank of America has thus produced) are not consistent with known signatures of Col. Goodall. The supposed witness to the says that she did not sign them and those are not her signatures. Bank of America says that it has lost the documents and refuses to produce them. Bank of America also refuses to provide any accounting of the funds.

What we have here is a clear case of criminal theft by Bank of America and their attorneys of an estate involving $2.5 million, almost all of which has been consumed by attorney's fees by Bank of America. The evidence points to the conclusion that the key signatures were forged by James R. Hastings, who was the Trust Administration Attorney for the Trust Department of the Bank of America and who prepared and witnessed and notarized the documents in this case. In order to cover up these crimes, Bank of America wants to donate the

entire estate to a charity, Guide Dogs for the Blind, leaving the actual Goodall heirs with nothing. The San Francisco Superior Court judge first wrongfully took jurisdiction over a case where there is no jurisdiction and then ruled in favor of Bank of America without allowing any discovery and with no fact hearing of any kind. The judge then made the case "Appeal Proof" by deliberately not signing the order denying rehearing until delaying two months to put it past the time to file a notice of appeal.

This document is prepared in Century Schoolbook New Bold 12 point with a word count of 8897 words.

Dated July 10, 2013 Respectfully Submitted,

Samuel H. Sloan
Administrator of Estate of
K. Michael Goodall with Will Annexed
461 Peachstone Terrace
San Rafael CA 94903
(415) 419-5980
917-659-3397
samhsloan@gmail.com

Court of Appeal, First Appellate District, Division Four - No. A137189

S208891

IN THE SUPREME COURT OF CALIFORNIA

En Banc

BANK OF AMERICA N. A., Plaintiff and Respondent,

v.

SAMUEL H. SLOAN, Objector and Appellant.

The petition for review is denied.

Chin, J., was recused and did not participate.

SUPREME COURT
FILED

APR 17 2013

Frank A. McGuire Clerk

Deputy

CANTIL-SAKAUYE

Chief Justice

COPY ORIGINAL

IN THE COURT OF APPEAL OF THE STATE OF CALIFORNIA

FIRST APPELLATE DISTRICT

DIVISION FOUR

FILED

JAN 15 2013

Court of Appeal - First App. Dist.
DIANA HERBERT
By ____________ DEPUTY

BANK OF AMERICA N.A., Plaintiff and Respondent, v. SAMUEL SLOAN, Objector and Appellant.	A137189 (San Francisco County Super. Ct. No. PTR99273030)

Appellant Samuel Sloan purports to appeal from an order that was issued by the San Francisco Superior Court concerning a trust.

The order at issue was filed on May 16, 2012, therefore appellant had no more than 180 days from that date to file his notice of appeal. (See Cal. Rules of Court, rule 8.104(a)(1)(C).) Appellant's notice of appeal, filed on November 21, 2012, is too late. Dismissal is mandatory. (See rule 8.104(b).)

The appeal is dismissed.

Dated JAN 15 2013 ____________ P.J.

COPY ORIGINAL

IN THE COURT OF APPEAL OF THE STATE OF CALIFORNIA

FIRST APPELLATE DISTRICT

DIVISION FOUR

FILED
FEB - 6 2013
Court of Appeal - First App. Dist.
DIANA HERBERT
By ____________ DEPUTY

BANK OF AMERICA N.A., Plaintiff and Respondent, v. SAMUEL SLOAN, Objector and Appellant.	A137189 (San Francisco County Super. Ct. No. PTR99273030)

BY THE COURT:

Appellant's petition for rehearing, filed on January 29, 2013, is denied.

Dated FEB - 6 2013 ____________ P.J.

Exhibit A

Order of San Francisco Superior Court dated May 15, 2012

MANATT, PHELPS & PHILLIPS, LLP
GARY D. ROTHSTEIN (Bar No. CA 143157)
One Embarcadero Center, 30th Floor
San Francisco, CA 94111
Telephone: (415) 291-7400
Facsimile: (415) 291-7474

Attorneys for ~~Petitioner~~ Trustee,
BANK OF AMERICA, N.A.

FILED
San Francisco County Superior Court
MAY 16 2012
CLERK OF THE COURT
BY: [signature] Deputy Clerk

SUPERIOR COURT OF THE STATE OF CALIFORNIA

FOR THE COUNTY OF SAN FRANCISCO

In the Matter of the Trust for Michael created under the Goodall Trust dated September 12, 1990.	Case No. PTR-99-273030 ~~[PROPOSED]~~ **ORDER RESULTING FROM HEARING ON MAY 7, 2012:** **(1) DENYING THE AMENDED PETITION OF SAM SLOAN FOR FORENSIC DOCUMENT EXAMINATION OF DOCUMENTS PURPORTED TO BE TRUST DOCUMENTS OF THE GOODALL FAMILY TRUST; AND** **(2) GRANTING BANK OF AMERICA, N.A.'S PETITION FOR DETERMINATION OF THE BENEFICIARIES TO WHOM TRUST PROPERTY SHALL PASS UPON TERMINATION OF TRUST** Hearing Date: May 7, 2012 Time: 9:00 a.m. Dept.: Probate (Room 204)

The following matters came on for hearing on May 7, 2012, at 9:00 a.m. in the Probate Department (Room 204) of the above-entitled Court, the Honorable Peter J. Busch, presiding: (a) Bank of America, N.A.'s Petition for Determination of the Beneficiaries to Whom Trust Property Shall Pass Upon Termination of Trust (the "Petition for Determination of Beneficiaries"); (b) Samuel Sloan's Objection to Petition for Determination of Beneficiaries and Request for Continuance of Hearing; (c) the Further Probate Opposition/Objection to Petition for

Determination of the Beneficiaries to Whom Trust Property Shall Pass Upon Termination of Trust Filed by Objector Samuel H. Sloan; (d) Samuel Sloan's Supplemental Objections to Petition for Determination of Beneficiaries and Request for Continuance of Hearing; (e) Petitioner Bank of America, N.A.'s Reply in Support of Petition for Determination of the Beneficiaries to Whom Trust Property Shall Pass upon Termination of Trust; (f) Sam Sloan's Further Supplemental Objections to Petition for Determination of Beneficiaries; (g) Sam Sloan's Objections to Evidence; (h) Guide Dogs for the Blind, Inc.'s Opposition to Sam Sloan's Further Supplemental Objections to Petition for Determination of Beneficiaries; (i) Petitioner Bank of America, N.A.'s Further Reply in Support of Petition for Determination of the Beneficiaries to Whom Trust Property Shall Pass Upon Termination of Trust; (j) Amended Petition of Sam Sloan for Forensic Document Examination of Documents Purported to be Trust Documents of the Goodall Family Trust (the "Amended Petition for Forensic Document Examination"); (k) Guide Dogs for the Blind, Inc.'s Opposition to Sam Sloan's Further Supplemental Objections to Petition for Determination of Beneficiaries; and (l) Petitioner Bank of America, N.A.'s Additional Reply in Support of Petition for Determination of the Beneficiaries to Whom Trust Property Shall Pass Upon Termination of Trust. Sam Ware appeared on behalf of Samuel Sloan. Alicia A. Adornato appeared on behalf of Guide Dogs for the Blind, Inc. Gary D. Rothstein appeared on behalf of Trustee, Bank of America, N.A. Samuel Sloan was present in the courtroom.

The Court finds the following:

(i) Notice of hearing of the Petition for Determination of Beneficiaries and notice of hearing of the Amended Petition for Forensic Document Examination have been given for the period of time and in the manner required by law;

(ii) Objections of Samuel Sloan to the validity of the Amendment to Goodall Trust dated August 24, 1994 (the "1994 Amendment") are time-barred under the statute of limitations of California Probate Code §16061.8. Consequently, good cause exists to overrule Samuel Sloan's objections to the validity of the 1994 Amendment. The 1994 Amendment is a valid, effective testamentary instrument executed by Kenneth F. Goodall and Rachel A. Goodall.

(iii) The production of the original 1994 Amendment is not necessary to determine the intent of Kenneth F. Goodall and Rachel A. Goodall with respect to the beneficiaries under the 1994 Amendment to whom the remainder of the Trust for Michael established under the 1994 Amendment shall pass due to the death of Michael Goodall because:

(a) The Notification by Trustee required under California Probate Code §16061.7 was served to Michael Goodall on October 5, 1999, and such Notification included the required warning advising Michael Goodall of the 120-day time period in which to challenge the validity of the 1994 Amendment;

(b) The 120-day time period in which to challenge the validity of the 1994 Amendment as prescribed by California Probate Code §16061.8 expired prior to Samuel Sloan asserting objections to the validity of the 1994 Amendment;

(c) Michael Goodall effectively adopted the 1994 Amendment when, in 1999 and 2000, respectively, he filed in this proceeding his Petition Re Determination That Particular Action By Beneficiary Does Not Constitute A Contest and his Petition for Removal of Trustee; and

(d) The original 1994 Amendment cannot say anything more relevant about the intent of Kenneth F. Goodall and Rachel A. Goodall with respect to the beneficiaries of the Trust for Michael than can a copy of the 1994 Amendment.

(iv) The best interpretation of the provisions of the 1994 Amendment with respect to determining the beneficiaries to whom the remaining assets of the Trust for Michael established thereunder shall pass due to the death of Michael Goodall, and of the intent of Kenneth F. Goodall and Rachel A. Goodall with respect to whom such beneficiaries are, is set forth in the Petition for Determination of Beneficiaries, to wit: such beneficiaries are determined pursuant to Section 6.3(d) of the 1994 Amendment, as follows:

(a) Twenty thousand dollars ($20,000) to each of the then living brothers and sisters of the trustor, RACHEL A. GOODALL;

(b) The remaining assets of the Trust for Michael to Guide Dogs for the Blind of Marin, Inc. of San Rafael, California.

///

IT IS THEREFORE ORDERED, JUDGED AND DECREED THAT:

1. The Amended Petition for Forensic Document Examination is denied.

2. The Petition for Determination of Beneficiaries is granted.

3. The Trust for Michael shall be distributed pursuant to Section 6.3(d) of the 1994 Amendment, as follows:

(a) Twenty thousand dollars ($20,000) to each of the then living brothers and sisters of the trustor, RACHEL A. GOODALL;

(b) The remaining assets of the Trust for Michael to Guide Dogs for the Blind of Marin, Inc. of San Rafael, California.

APPROVED AS TO FORM AND SUBSTANCE:

Dated: May 11, 2012

Manatt, Phelps, & Phillips, LLP

By: [signature]
Gary D. Rothstein
Attorneys for Bank of America, N.A., Trustee

Dated: ______________

____
Sam Ware
Attorney for Samuel Sloan

Dated: ______________

Reed Smith LLP

By: ______________
Alicia A. Adornato
Attorneys for Guide Dogs for the Blind, Inc.

Date: ______________

____
Judge of the Superior Court

IT IS THEREFORE ORDERED, JUDGED AND DECREED THAT:

1. The Amended Petition for Forensic Document Examination is denied.

2. The Petition for Determination of Beneficiaries is granted.

3. The Trust for Michael shall be distributed pursuant to Section 6.3(d) of the 1994 Amendment, as follows:

(a) Twenty thousand dollars ($20,000) to each of the then living brothers and sisters of the trustor, RACHEL A. GOODALL;

(b) The remaining assets of the Trust for Michael to Guide Dogs for the Blind of Marin, Inc. of San Rafael, California.

APPROVED AS TO FORM ~~AND SUBSTANCE~~:

Dated: ______________________ Manatt, Phelps, & Phillips, LLP

By: ______________________
Gary D. Rothstein
Attorneys for Bank of America, N.A., Trustee

Dated: ______________________

____
Sam Ware
Attorney for Samuel Sloan

Dated: ______________________ Reed Smith LLP

By: ______________________
Alicia A. Adornato
Attorneys for Guide Dogs for the Blind, Inc.

Date: ______________________

____
Judge of the Superior Court

IT IS THEREFORE ORDERED, JUDGED AND DECREED THAT:

1. The Amended Petition for Forensic Document Examination is denied.

2. The Petition for Determination of Beneficiaries is granted.

3. The Trust for Michael shall be distributed pursuant to Section 6.3(d) of the 1994 Amendment, as follows:

(a) Twenty thousand dollars ($20,000) to each of the then living brothers and sisters of the trustor, RACHEL A. GOODALL;

(b) The remaining assets of the Trust for Michael to Guide Dogs for the Blind of Marin, Inc. of San Rafael, California.

APPROVED AS TO FORM AND SUBSTANCE:

Dated: ______________________ Manatt, Phelps, & Phillips, LLP

By: ______________________
Gary D. Rothstein
Attorneys for Bank of America, N.A., Trustee

Dated: ______________________ ______________________
Sam Ware
Attorney for Samuel Sloan

Dated: May 10, 2012 Reed Smith LLP

By: [signature]
Alicia A. Adornato
Attorneys for Guide Dogs for the Blind, Inc.

Date: 5/15/2012 [signature]
Judge of the Superior Court

Exhibit B

Order of San Francisco Superior Court dated September 27, 2012

MANATT, PHELPS & PHILLIPS, LLP
GARY D. ROTHSTEIN (Bar No. CA 143157)
One Embarcadero Center, 30th Floor
San Francisco, CA 94111
Telephone: (415) 291-7400
Facsimile: (415) 291-7474

Attorneys for Petitioner,
BANK OF AMERICA, N.A.

ENDORSED
FILED
San Francisco County Superior Court

SEP 27 2012

CLERK OF THE COURT
By NOELIA RIVERA
Deputy Clerk

SUPERIOR COURT OF THE STATE OF CALIFORNIA

FOR THE COUNTY OF SAN FRANCISCO

In the Matter of the Trust for Michael created under the Goodall Trust dated September 12, 1990.	Case No. PTR-99-273030 **[PROPOSED] ORDER DENYING SAM SLOAN'S AMENDED NOTICE OF MOTION AND MOTION TO RECONSIDER [ERRONEOUSLY CAPTIONED EARLIER AS MOTION TO COMPEL PRODUCTION OF DOCUMENTS]** Hearing Date: July 19, 2012 Time: 2:00 p.m. Dept.: Probate (Room 204)

The following matters came on for hearing on July 19, 2012, at 2:00 p.m. in the Probate Department (Room 204) of the above-entitled Court, the Honorable Peter J. Busch, presiding: (a) Sam Sloan's Notice of Motion and Motion to Reconsider [Erroneously Captioned Earlier as Motion to Compel Production of Documents] and Declaration of Sloan in Support Thereof ("Sloan's Motion to Reconsider"); (b) Declaration of David S. Moore; (c) Bank of America, N.A.'s Opposition to Sam Sloan's Amended Notice of Motion and Motion to Reconsider [Erroneously Captioned Earlier as Motion to Compel Production of Documents]; (d) Declaration of Gary D. Rothstein in Support of Bank of America, N.A.'S Opposition to Sam Sloan's Amended Notice of Motion and Motion for Reconsideration; (e) Guide Dogs for the Blind, Inc.'s Joinder in Bank of America, N.A.'s Response to Sam Sloan's Motion to Reconsider;

and (f) Sam Sloan's Reply Memorandum Regarding Motion to Reconsider, and Declaration of Sam Ware in support thereof. Sam Ware appeared on behalf of Samuel Sloan. Alicia A. Adornato appeared on behalf of Guide Dogs for the Blind, Inc. Gary D. Rothstein appeared on behalf of Trustee, Bank of America, N.A. Samuel Sloan was present in the courtroom.

On July 18, 2012, the Court issued a Tentative Ruling with respect to the foregoing documents, which stated, in relevant part, as follows:

> "The Motion to Reconsider (mistitled as "Motion to Compel Production of Documents and Further Deposition") is denied. The moving party has not presented new facts or circumstances within the meaning of C.C.P. section 1008, and, in any event, to the extent any of moving party's submissions was properly considered new facts or circumstances, it would not lead the Court to change its ruling."

Having considered the foregoing documents, all papers submitted in support thereof, all papers submitted in opposition thereof, all other papers in the Court file in this matter, and the argument of counsel presented at the hearing, the Court makes the following findings:

(i) Notice of hearing of Sloan's Motion to Reconsider has been given for the period of time and in the manner required by law;

(ii) Good cause exists to adopt the Tentative Ruling as the Court's final order; and

(iii) Good cause does not exist for the Court to impose sanctions against Sam Sloan or Sam Ware at this time.

///

///

///

///

///

///

///

///

///

IT IS THEREFORE ORDERED, JUDGED AND DECREED THAT:

1. Sloan's Motion to Reconsider is denied; and

2. No sanctions are imposed at this time.

APPROVED AS TO FORM AND SUBSTANCE:

Dated: July 27, 2012

Manatt, Phelps, & Phillips, LLP

By: Gary D. Rothstein
Gary D. Rothstein
Attorneys for Bank of America, N.A., Trustee

Dated: ____________________

____
Sam Ware
Attorney for Samuel Sloan

Dated: ____________________

Reed Smith LLP

By: ____________________
Alicia A. Adornato
Attorneys for Guide Dogs for the Blind, Inc.

Date: ____________________

____
Judge of the Superior Court

IT IS THEREFORE ORDERED. JUDGED AND DECREED THAT:

1. Sloan's Motion to Reconsider is denied: and

2. No sanctions are imposed at this time.

APPROVED AS TO FORM AND SUBSTANCE:

Dated: ______________________ Manatt, Phelps, & Phillips, LLP

By: ______________________
Gary D. Rothstein
Attorneys for Bank of America, N.A., Trustee

Dated: 7/27/12 ______________________
Sam Ware
Attorney for Samuel Sloan

Dated: ______________________ Reed Smith LLP

By: ______________________
Alicia A. Adornato
Attorneys for Guide Dogs for the Blind, Inc.

Date: ______________________ ______________________
Judge of the Superior Court

IT IS THEREFORE ORDERED, JUDGED AND DECREED THAT:

1. Sloan's Motion to Reconsider is denied; and

2. No sanctions are imposed at this time.

APPROVED AS TO FORM AND SUBSTANCE:

Dated: ____________________ Manatt, Phelps, & Phillips, LLP

By: ____________________
Gary D. Rothstein
Attorneys for Bank of America, N.A., Trustee

Dated: ____________________

____
Sam Ware
Attorney for Samuel Sloan

Dated: July 27, 2012 Reed Smith LLP

By: Alicia Adornato
Alicia A. Adornato
Attorneys for Guide Dogs for the Blind, Inc.

Date: 9/26/2012

PETER J. BUSCH
____
Judge of the Superior Court

Exhibit C

Order of San Francisco Superior Court dated November 15, 2012

MC-053

ATTORNEY OR PARTY WITHOUT ATTORNEY (*Name, state bar number, and address*):
Sam Ware 105005
700 Larkspur Landing Cir #199
Larkspur CA 94939

TELEPHONE NO.: 415 464 4872 FAX NO. (*Optional*):
E-MAIL ADDRESS (*Optional*):
ATTORNEY FOR (*Name*): pro per

FOR COURT USE ONLY

FILED
Superior Court of California
County of San Francisco
NOV 15 2012
CLERK OF THE COURT
BY: Rosie Noguera
Deputy Clerk

SUPERIOR COURT OF CALIFORNIA, COUNTY OF San Francisco
STREET ADDRESS: 400 McAllister St
MAILING ADDRESS:
CITY AND ZIP CODE: San Francisco CA
BRANCH NAME:

CASE NAME:
In Re Goodall Trust

CASE NUMBER:
PTR 99 273030

ORDER GRANTING ATTORNEY'S MOTION TO BE RELIEVED AS COUNSEL—CIVIL

HEARING DATE: October 29, 2012
DEPT.: 204 TIME: 10:30 am
BEFORE HON.: Peter Busch
DATE ACTION FILED: 12/21/99
TRIAL DATE: none

1. The motion of (*name of attorney*): Sam Ware
to be relieved as counsel of record for (*name of client*): Samuel Sloan
a party to this action or proceeding, came on regularly for hearing at the date, time, and place indicated above.

2. The following persons were present at the hearing:
Sam Ware, Samuel Sloan, and Arden Van Upp

FINDINGS

3. Attorney has
   a. [ ] personally served the client with papers in support of this motion.
   b. [✓] served client by mail and submitted a declaration establishing that the service requirements of California Rules of Court, rule 3.1362, have been satisfied.

4. Attorney has shown sufficient reasons why the motion to be relieved as counsel should be granted and why the attorney has brought a motion under Code of Civil Procedure section 284(2) instead of filing a consent under section 284(1).

ORDER

5. Attorney is relieved as counsel of record for client
   a. [ ] effective upon the filing of the proof of service of this signed order upon the client.
   b. [✓] effective on (*specify date*): 10/29/2012

6. The client's [✓] current [ ] last known address and telephone number:
461 Peachstone Ter., San Rafael CA 94930 (415) 419-5980

If the client's current address is known, service on the client must hereafter be made at that address unless otherwise ordered in item 13. If the current address is not known, service must be made according to Code of Civil Procedure section 1011 (b) and rule 3.252 of the California Rules of Court.

7. a. The next scheduled hearing in this action or proceeding is set for (*date, time, and place*):
PJB November 15, 2012 Dept 204 of the above Court
   b. The hearing will concern (*subject matter*):
Motion for Sanctions

NOTICE TO CLIENT
You or your new attorney, if any, must prepare for and attend this hearing.

CASE NAME: In Re Goodall Trust	CASE NUMBER: PTR 99 273030

8. The following additional hearings and other proceedings (including discovery matters) are set in this action *(describe the date, time, place, and subject matter of each)*:
none

9. The trial in this action or proceeding:
a. [✓] is not yet set.
b. [ ] is set for *(specify date, time, and place)*:

10. Client is hereby notified of the following effects this order may have upon parties.

NOTICE TO CLIENT

Your present attorney will no longer be representing you. You may not in most cases represent yourself if you are one of the parties on the following list:

- A guardian
- A conservator
- A trustee
- A personal representative
- A probate fiduciary
- A corporation
- A guardian ad litem
- An unincorporated association

If you are one of these parties, YOU SHOULD IMMEDIATELY SEEK LEGAL ADVICE REGARDING LEGAL REPRESENTATION. Failure to retain an attorney may lead to an order striking the pleadings or to the entry of a default judgment.

11. Client is notified that, if the client will be representing himself or herself, the client shall be solely responsible for the case.

NOTICE TO CLIENT WHO WILL BE UNREPRESENTED

You will not have an attorney representing you. You may wish to seek legal assistance. If you do not have a new attorney to represent you in this action or proceeding, and you are legally permitted to do so, you will be representing yourself. It will be your responsibility to comply with all court rules and applicable laws. If you fail to do so, or fail to appear at hearings, action may be taken against you. You may lose your case.

12. Client is notified that it is the client's duty to keep the court informed at all times of the client's current address.

NOTICE TO CLIENT WHO WILL BE UNREPRESENTED

The court needs to know how to contact you. If you do not keep the court and other parties informed of your current address and telephone number, they will not be able to send you notices of actions that may affect you, including actions that may adversely affect your interests or result in your losing the case.

13. The court further orders *(specify)*:

Date: 11/15/2012

Peter J B[signature]
JUDGE OR JUDICIAL OFFICER
PETER J. BUSCH

Exhibit D

Order of San Francisco Superior Court dated November 26, 2012

SAM WARE (State Bar No. 105005)
700 Larkspur Landing Circle, #199
Larkspur, CA 94939

Telephone 415-464-4872

E-mail sam@samware.us

Sanctions Respondent, Pro per

SUPERIOR COURT OF THE STATE OF CALIFORNIA

COUNTY OF SAN FRANCISCO

In the Matter of the Trust for Michael created under the Goodall Trust dated September 12, 1990	Case No. PTR-99-273030 Order Denying Motion for Sanctions Hrg Date: November 15, 2012 Time: 2:00 PM Department: 204

The court having considered Bank of America's motion for sanctions on November 15, 2012,

It is hereby ordered that the motion is denied.

Date: 11/21/2012

Judge of the Superior Court

Approved as to Form:

Attorneys for Bank of America

Exhibit E

Register of Actions in Marin County Probate Court in Estate of K. Michael Goodall, Case No. 1100596

MARIN SUPERIOR COURT OF CALIFORNIA, COUNTY OF MARIN		
MICHAEL GOODALL, ESTATE OF Decedent(s) VS. Trustee(s)	DATE FILED:	2/1/2011
	CASE TYPE:	Probate
	CASE SUBTYPE:	Decedent - Estate
	DATE OF LAST ACTIVITY:	9/24/2012
	DATE/TIME RUN:	1/28/2013 11:50am
REGISTER OF ACTIONS	CASE NUMBER:	PRO 1100596

LVED PERSON/PARTY AND ATTORNEY SUMMARY:

GOODALL, K. MICHAEL is the Decedent and is represented by:

BANK OF AMERICA N.A. is the Trustee and is represented by: ROTHSTEIN, GARY D.

SLOAN, SAMUEL H. is the Personal Representative and is represented by: PRO PER

GUIDE DOGS FOR THE BLIND, INC. is the Other and is represented by: ADORNATO, ALICIA

ISTER OF ACTIONS:

011 CASE OPEN / ACTIVE STATUS Hon. Verna A. Adams

011 FILING FEE PROCESSED: PREP, SAMUEL SLOAN - 395.00

011 COMPLAINT/FIRST PAPER PETITION FOR PROBATE OF WILL AND FOR LETTERS TESTAMENTARY. $395.00 PAID.

011 HEARING CONFIRMED FOR: 03/07/2011 AT: 08:30 AM FOR APPEARANCE TYPE: PROB IN DEPARTMENT: D01

011 HEARING CONFIRMED FOR: 02/01/2013 AT: 09:00 AM FOR APPEARANCE TYPE: CSCM IN DEPARTMENT: Z7

2011 PROOF OF PUBLICATION FILED MARINSCOPE; FEB.9, 16, AND 23, 2011

011 DUTIES AND LIABILITIES OF PERSONAL REPRESENTATIVE FILED, BY SAMUEL H. SLOAN

011 MINUTE ORDER POSTED - Appearance: 3/7/2011 at 08:30 AM for PETITION FOR PROBATE

JUDGE/PROTEM/REFEREE VERNA A. ADAMS , REPORTER NOT REPORTED , DEP CLK VITA JOHANSON

PLAINTIFF/PETITIONER SAMUEL SLOAN IS PRESENT IN PRO PER

TENTATIVE RULING CONTINUED.

CONTINUED TO MARCH 21, 2011 FOR NOTICE TO ALTERNATIVE EXECUTOR.

HEARING CONTINUED TO: 03/21/2011 AT: 08:30 AM FOR APPEARANCE TYPE: PROB IN DEPARTMENT: D01 FROM DATE: 03/07/2011 FROM TIME: 08:30 AM FROM APPEARANCE TYPE: PROB FROM DEPARTMENT: D01

ENTERED BY: VJ

2011 CREDITOR'S CLAIM BANK OF AMERICA: $14,451.19

2011 CREDITOR'S CLAIM BANK OF AMERICA: $11,109.61

2011 MINUTE ORDER POSTED - Appearance: 3/21/2011 at 08:30 AM for PETITION FOR PROBATE

JUDGE/PROTEM/REFEREE VERNA A. ADAMS , REPORTER CATHY HEEFNER , DEP CLK JULIE WITHEY

ATTORNEY SAMUEL H. SLOAN APPEARED FOR HIMSELF AS PERSONAL REPRESENTATIVE

APPEARANCE BY ROY HOPPE EXECUTOR

TENTATIVE RULING : APPEARANCE IS REQUIRED. IF THERE IS NO APPEARANCE THEN THE MATTER IS OFF CALENDAR

THE COURT NOTES THE PROOF OF SERVICE TO BANK OF AMERICA HAS BEEN FILED.

IT IS ORDERED: THE COURT ACCEPTS THE RESIGNATION OF MR. HOPPE AS EXECUTOR AND APPOINTS SAMUEL H. SLOAN.

THE TENTATIVE RULING IS AFFIRMED AND MADE FINAL.

ORDER SIGNED IN OPEN COURT

ENTERED BY: JW

3/21/2011 ORDER FOR PROBATE APPOINTING SAMUEL H. SLOAN ADMINISTRATOR WITH WILL ANNEXED WITH FULL AUTHORITY. SIGNED BY JUDGE VERNA A. ADAMS

3/21/2011 WILL DATED: 1/15/04 FILED

3/21/2011 LETTERS OF ADMINISTRATION WITH WILL ANNEXED WITH FULL AUTHORITY: SAMUEL H. SLOAN APPOINTED

3/29/2011 CREDITOR'S CLAIM $974.27 PACIFIC GAS AND ELECTRIC COMPANY

4/12/2011 HEARING CONFIRMED FOR: 08/24/2011 AT: 09:00 AM FOR APPEARANCE TYPE: PROB IN DEPARTMENT: Z8

4/12/2011 HEARING CONFIRMED FOR: 04/25/2012 AT: 09:00 AM FOR APPEARANCE TYPE: PROB IN DEPARTMENT: Z8

5/20/2011 HEARING CONFIRMED FOR: 05/20/2011 AT: 09:00 AM FOR APPEARANCE TYPE: PROB IN DEPARTMENT: D07

5/20/2011 MINUTE ORDER POSTED

EX PARTE MINUTE ORDER

JUDGE/PROTEM/REFEREE HARVEY E. GOLDFINE , REPORTER ELAINE NINKOVICH , DEP CLK CHRIS HAHN

APPEARANCE BY SAMUEL SLOAN, ADMINISTRATOR WITH WILL ANNEXED, PETITIONER.

APPEARANCE BY GARY ROTHSTEIN, TRUSTEE, BANK OF AMERICA, APPEARING BY COURT CALL.

APPEARANCE BY MATTHEW URBACH, TRUSTEE, BANK OF AMERICA. APPEARING BY COURT CALL.

NOTICE GIVEN AS REQUIRED BY LAW

MR. ROTHSTEIN REPORTS HE HAS RECEIVED A COPY OF THE PETITION AND TEMPORARY RESTRAINING ORDER WITH REGARD TO THE TRUST CREATED BY DECEDANT'S PARENTS FOR THE DECEDANT.

MR. ROTHSTEIN FURTHER REPORTS HE HAS BEEN INFORMED THAT THE PROPERTY WAS VACATED AND ITS CONTENTS, SOME OF WHICH ARE PART OF THE TRUST, WERE REMOVED AND PUT IN STORAGE AT AN AUCTION HOUSE.

MR. ROTHSTEIN STATES HIS BELIEF THAT THE HOME IS AN ASSET OF THE TRUST. THIS MATTER IS GOING TO BE HEARD IN THE SAN FRANCISCO COUNTY SUPERIOR COURT ON MAY 25, 2011.

MR. ROTHSTEIN HAS NO OBJECTION TO ORDER SHORTENING TIME.

MR. SLOAN REPORTS THAT PROPERTY BELONGING TO ROY HOPPE, AN ALLEGED BENEFICIARY OF THE WILL, WAS REMOVED AND THAT MR. HOPPE IS NOW HOMELESS.

MR. SLOAN STATES HE RECEIVED NO NOTICE OF INTENT TO REMOVE PROPERTY FROM THE HOME AND, IN HIS OPINION, ANY LEGAL ACTION MUST BE TAKEN IN THE COUNTY WHERE THE PROPERTY IS LOCATED.

THE COURT MAKES THE FOLLOWING FINDINGS AND ORDERS:

COURT GRANTS ORDER SHORTENING TIME.

COURT INFORMS MR. SLOAN THAT IT IS HIS RESPONSIBILITY TO SUBMIT ORDER SHORTENING TIME AND CITATION TO THE AUCTION HOUSE.

THIS MATTER IS CONTINUED TO JUNE 13, 2011 AT 8:30 AM IN DEPARTMENT "H" BEFORE JUDGE ADAMS FOR CONSIDERATION OF RESTRAINING ORDER AND FURTHER PROCEEDINGS.

HEARING CONTINUED TO: 06/13/2011 AT: 08:30 AM FOR APPEARANCE TYPE: PROB IN DEPARTMENT: D01 FROM DATE: 05/20/2011 FROM TIME: 09:00 AM FROM APPEARANCE TYPE: PROB FROM DEPARTMENT: D07

MR. ROTHSTEIN ACCEPTS SERVICE OF NOTICE AS TO NEXT HEARING ON BEHALF OF BANK OF AMERICA.

ENTERED BY: CHRIS HAHN

/2011 IT IS ORDERED: ORDER SHORTENING TIME ON PREP'S MTN. TO RECOVER ESTATE PROPERTY TO BE HEARD ON 6/13/11 AT 8:30AM IN DEPT. H. SIGNED BY COMM. HARVEY E. GOLDFINE

/2011 MINUTE ORDER POSTED - Appearance: 6/13/2011 at 08:30 AM for OTHER

JUDGE/PROTEM/REFEREE VERNA A. ADAMS , REPORTER NOT REPORTED , DEP CLK J. CHARIFA

APPEARANCE BY PERSONAL REPRESENTATIVE, SAM SLOAN.

APPEARANCE BY ROY HOPPE, BENEFECIARY OF THE ESTATE.

COUNSEL INDICATES THAT PROPERTY HAS BEEN RETURNED.

IT IS ORDERED: OFF CALENDAR. MATTER HAS BEEN RESOLVED.

ISSUES RAISED BY MR. SLOAN REGARDING RACHEL GOODALL AND THE DIFFICULTY OF RETAINING INFORMATION FROM BANK OF AMERICA ON THE STATUS OF THE MONEY, ARE NOT BEFORE THE COURTAT THIS TIME. MR. SLOAN IS DIRECTED TO FILE AN APPROPRIATE PETITION WITH THE COURT IF HE WISHES TO PURSUE THESE ISSUES.

ENTERED BY: JC

/2011 HEARING CONFIRMED FOR: 09/26/2011 AT: 08:30 AM FOR APPEARANCE TYPE: PROB IN DEPARTMENT: D01

2011 HEARING CONFIRMED FOR: 08/22/2011 AT: 08:30 AM FOR APPEARANCE TYPE: PROB IN DEPARTMENT: D01

/2011 MINUTE ORDER POSTED - Appearance: 8/22/2011 at 08:30 AM for PETITION

JUDGE/PROTEM/REFEREE VERNA A. ADAMS , REPORTER NOT REPORTED , DEP CLK VITA JOHANSON

NO APPEARANCE BY OR FOR THE PARTIES

THE MATTER IS NOT HEARD OR REPORTED. THE TENTATIVE RULING IS FINAL.

RULING- IF NO OBJECTIONS ARE RAISED THEN THE MATTER IS PRE-GRANTED AND NO APPEARANCE IS NECESSARY.

PETITION GRANTED.

ENTERED BY: VJ

/2011 IT IS ORDERED: ORDER ON PETITION FOR AUTHORITY TO ENTER INTO CONTINGENCY FEE AGREEMENT GRANTED. SIGNED BY JUDGE VERNA A. ADAMS

2011 APPEARANCE MOVED TO: 10/26/2011 AT: 09:00 AM FOR APPEARANCE TYPE: PROB IN DEPARTMENT: Z8 MOVE REASON: * FROM DATE: 08/24/2011 FROM TIME: 09:00 AM FROM APPEARANCE TYPE: PROB FROM DEPARTMENT: Z8

/2011 HEARING CONFIRMED FOR: 12/27/2011 AT: 08:30 AM FOR APPEARANCE TYPE: PROB IN DEPARTMENT: D01

/2011 FILING FEE PROCESSED: TRUS, BANK OF AMERICA N.A. - 395.00

/2011 DEMURRER TO SAMUEL H. SLOAN'S PETITION UNDER CA. PROB. CODE SEC. 850 TO RECOVER ESTATE PROPERTY FILED BY BANK OF AMERICA, N.A.. $395.00 PAID.

/2011 MINUTE ORDER POSTED - Appearance: 9/26/2011 at 08:30 AM for PETITION

JUDGE/PROTEM/REFEREE COMM. RANDOLPH E. HEUBACH , REPORTER NOT REPORTED , DEP CLK G. COMPTON

APPEARANCE BY SAMUEL SLOAN

APPEARANCE BY BENEFICIARIES OF THE ESTATE, FRANK THORNALLY AND ROY HOPPE

SAMUEL SLOAN CALLED OBJECTS TO THE COURT'S TENTATIVE RULING.

MR. SLOAN REQUESTS FOR AN ACCOUNTING OF THE FUNDS.

THE COURT NOTES THAT THERE'S A PENDING TRUST ACTION IN SAN FRANCISCO AND THE DEMURRER NEEDS TO BE RESOLVED BEFORE THIS PETITIONER IS HEARD.

IT IS ORDERED: MATTER CONTINUED TO 12/27/11 @ 8:30 A.M. TO POTENTIALLY BE SET FOLLOWING RULING ON DERMURRER.

THE TENTATIVE RULING IS AFFIRMED AND MADE FINAL.

TENTATIVE RULING CONTINUED.

ENTERED BY: G. COMPTON

11/10/2011 APPEARANCE MOVED TO: 05/09/2012 AT: 09:00 AM FOR APPEARANCE TYPE: PROB IN DEPARTMENT: Z8 MOVE REASON: * FROM DATE: 10/26/2011 FROM TIME: 09:00 AM FROM APPEARANCE TYPE: PROB FROM DEPARTMENT: Z8

11/10/2011 APPEARANCE MOVED TO: 07/11/2012 AT: 09:00 AM FOR APPEARANCE TYPE: PROB IN DEPARTMENT: Z8 MOVE REASON: * FROM DATE: 04/25/2012 FROM TIME: 09:00 AM FROM APPEARANCE TYPE: PROB FROM DEPARTMENT: Z8

12/27/2011 MINUTE ORDER POSTED - Appearance: 12/27/2011 at 08:30 AM for MOTION

JUDGE/PROTEM/REFEREE COMM. RANDOLPH E. HEUBACH , REPORTER MAUREEN STEGER , DEP CLK G. COMPTON

APPEARANCE BY ADMINISTRATOR, SAMUEL SLOAN

NO APPEARANCE BY OR FOR THE TRUSTEE, BANK OF AMERICA

MR. SLOAN OBJECTS TO THE CONTINUANCE OF HIS MOTION FOR TO RECOVER ESTATE PROPERTY AND REQUESTS FOR HIS PETITION TO BE GRANTED. STATES THAT HE ONLY AGREED TO THE CONTINUANCE FOR THE DEMURRER.

TENTATIVE RULING CONTINUED.

IT IS ORDERED: CASE IS CONTINUED TO 02/21/12 @ 8:30 A.M. BY STIPULATION.

HEARING CONTINUED TO: 02/21/2012 AT: 08:30 AM FOR APPEARANCE TYPE: PROB IN DEPARTMENT: D01 FROM DATE: 12/27/2011 FROM TIME: 08:30 AM FROM APPEARANCE TYPE: PROB FROM DEPARTMENT: D01

ENTERED BY: G. COMPTON

2/21/2012 MINUTE ORDER POSTED - Appearance: 2/21/2012 at 08:30 AM for MOTION

DEPARTMENT H MATTER CALENDARED IN DEPARTMENT A.

JUDGE/PROTEM/REFEREE HARVEY E. GOLDFINE , REPORTER NOT REPORTED , DEP CLK CHRIS HAHN

NO APPEARANCE BY OR FOR THE PARTIES

TENTATIVE RULING: CONTINUED TO 3-19-2012 AT 8:30 AM BY STIPULATION.

HEARING CONTINUED TO: 03/19/2012 AT: 08:30 AM FOR APPEARANCE TYPE: PROB IN DEPARTMENT: D01 FROM DATE: 02/21/2012 FROM TIME: 08:30 AM FROM APPEARANCE TYPE: PROB FROM DEPARTMENT: D01

ENTERED BY: CHRIS HAHN

012 FILING FEE PROCESSED: OTHR, GUIDE DOGS FOR THE BLIND, INC. - 395.00

012 OPPOSITION TO MOTION FOR ORDER TO RELEASE LODGED DOCUMENTS PURPORTED TO BE THE ORIGINAL WILLS DECEDENTS KENNETH F. GOODALL AND RACHEL A. GOODALL FOR FORENSIC DOCUMENT EXAMINATION FILED BY GUIDE DOGS FOR THE BLIND, INC. $395.00 PAID.

2012 REPLY TO BANK OF AMERICA'S ATTEMPT AT DEMURRER FILED BY SAMUEL H. SLOAN.

2012 MINUTE ORDER POSTED - Appearance: 3/19/2012 at 08:30 AM for MOTION

JUDGE/PROTEM/REFEREE VERNA A. ADAMS , REPORTER NOT REPORTED , DEP CLK VITA JOHANSON

NO APPEARANCE BY OR FOR THE PARTIES

TENTATIVE RULING CONTINUED.

IT IS ORDERED: CONTINUED TO APRIL 2, 2012 FOR FURTHER REVIEW

HEARING CONTINUED TO: 04/02/2012 AT: 08:30 AM FOR APPEARANCE TYPE: PROB IN DEPARTMENT: D01 FROM DATE: 03/19/2012 FROM TIME: 08:30 AM FROM APPEARANCE TYPE: PROB FROM DEPARTMENT: D01

ENTERED BY: VJ

2012 IT IS ORDERED: ORDER TO CONTINUE HEARING FROM 4/2/12 TO 4/16/12 GRANTED. SIGNED BY JUDGE VERNA A. ADAMS

012 MINUTE ORDER POSTED - Appearance: 4/2/2012 at 08:30 AM for MOTION

JUDGE/PROTEM/REFEREE VERNA A. ADAMS , REPORTER NOT REPORTED , DEP CLK VITA JOHANSON

NO APPEARANCE BY OR FOR THE PARTIES

TENTATIVE RULING CONTINUED.

IT IS ORDERED: CONTINUED TO APRIL 16, 2012 BY STIPULATION

HEARING CONTINUED TO: 04/16/2012 AT: 08:30 AM FOR APPEARANCE TYPE: PROB IN DEPARTMENT: D01 FROM DATE: 04/02/2012 FROM TIME: 08:30 AM FROM APPEARANCE TYPE: PROB FROM DEPARTMENT: D01

ENTERED BY: VJ

2012 MINUTE ORDER POSTED - Appearance: 4/16/2012 at 08:30 AM for MOTION

JUDGE/PROTEM/REFEREE VERNA A. ADAMS , REPORTER NOT REPORTED , DEP CLK VITA JOHANSON

ATTORNEY ALICIA ADORNATO APPEARED FOR GUIDE DOGS FOR THE BLIND

ATTORNEY GARY ROTHSTEIN APPEARED FOR TRUSTEE BANK OF AMERICA

APPEARANCE BY ADMINISTRATOR SAMUEL SLOAN, SELF REPRESENTED LITIGANT

MATTER COMES BEFORE THE COURT ON AN APPEARANCE IS REQUIRED TENTATIVE RULING

THE MATTER IS HEARD AND ARGUED

MATTER IS SUBMITTED

BANK OF AMERICA'S REQUEST FOR JUDICIAL NOTICE FILED 09-22-2011 IS GRANTED, PER EVIDENCE CODE SECTIONS 452 AND 453.

IT IS ORDERED: THE DEMURRER IS SUSTANED WITHOUT LEAVE TO AMEND AND THE SECTION 850 PETITION IS DENIED WITHOUT PREJUDICE.

THE MOTION FOR AN ORDER TO RELEASE DOCUMENTS TO A FORENSIC DOCUMENT EXAMINER: THAT MOTION IS DENIED.

PETITION DENIED.

CASE DISPOSED IN ENTIRETY

CASE RE-OPENED / ACTIVE (CASE DISPOSED ENTRY IS CLERICAL ERROR)

ENTERED BY: VJ

4/26/2012 IT IS ORDERED: ORDER RESULTING FROM HEARING ON APRIL 16, 2012 GRANTED. SIGNED BY JUDGE VERNA A. ADAMS (SEE FILE FOR FULL DETAILS OF ORDER)

5/15/2012 APPEARANCE MOVED TO: 09/19/2012 AT: 09:00 AM FOR APPEARANCE TYPE: PROB IN DEPARTMENT: Z8 MOVE REASON: * FROM DATE: 05/09/2012 FROM TIME: 09:00 AM FROM APPEARANCE TYPE: PROB FROM DEPARTMENT: Z8

9/24/2012 APPEARANCE MOVED TO: 11/14/2012 AT: 09:00 AM FOR APPEARANCE TYPE: PROB IN DEPARTMENT: Z8 MOVE REASON: * FROM DATE: 09/19/2012 FROM TIME: 09:00 AM FROM APPEARANCE TYPE: PROB FROM DEPARTMENT: Z8

Exhibit F

Register of Actions in Marin County Superior Court Unlawful Detainer Proceedings Case Numbers Civ 1203665 and Civ 1204541 and Order of Dismissal

MARIN SUPERIOR COURT OF CALIFORNIA, COUNTY OF MARIN		
BANK OF AMERICA, N.A. Plaintiff(s) VS. SAMUEL H. SLOAN, ET. AL. Defendant(s)	DATE FILED:	8/8/2012
	CASE TYPE:	Civil Complaint
	CASE SUBTYPE:	Unlawful Detainer
	DATE OF LAST ACTIVITY:	12/31/2012
	DATE/TIME RUN:	1/28/2013 12:02pm
REGISTER OF ACTIONS	CASE NUMBER:	CIV 1203665

INVOLVED PERSON/PARTY AND ATTORNEY SUMMARY:

BANK OF AMERICA, N.A. is the Plaintiff and is represented by: LOPEZ, ZAHER ; ROTHSTEIN, GARY D.

SLOAN, SAMUEL H. is the Defendant and is represented by: PRO PER

HOPPE, ROY is the Defendant and is represented by: PRO PER

THORNALLY, FRANK is the Defendant and is represented by: PRO PER

KIMURA, KAYO is the Defendant and is represented by: PRO PER

REGISTER OF ACTIONS:

8/8/2012	CASE OPEN / ACTIVE STATUS Hon. Roy O. Chernus
8/8/2012	CASE MARKED AS CONFIDENTIAL
8/8/2012	FULL NAME OF PLAINTIFF: BANK OF AMERICA, N.A., TRUSTEE OF THE TRUST FOR MICHAEL CREATED UNDER THE GOODALL TRUST DATED SEPTEMBER 12, 1990
8/8/2012	FILING FEE PROCESSED: PLTF, BANK OF AMERICA, N.A. - 240.00
8/8/2012	COMPLAINT/FIRST PAPER AMOUNT DOES NOT EXCEED $10,000
8/8/2012	SUMMONS ISSUED AND FILED
8/9/2012	AMENDED COMPLAINT FILED (1ST) BY ATTY GARY ROTHSTEIN; ZAHER LOPEZ OBO PLTF. (NO ADDL PARTIES)
8/9/2012	SUMMONS ISSUED (1ST AMENDED) AND FILED
8/9/2012	HEARING CONFIRMED FOR: 12/31/2012 AT: 08:30 AM FOR APPEARANCE TYPE: OSCH IN DEPARTMENT: D06
8/9/2012	HEARING CONFIRMED FOR: 12/31/2013 AT: 09:00 AM FOR APPEARANCE TYPE: CSCM IN DEPARTMENT: Z7
8/17/2012	ANSWER DEFT, SAMUEL SLOAN
8/17/2012	FILING FEE PROCESSED: DEFT, SAMUEL SLOAN - 225.00
8/20/2012	UD PROPERTY LOCATION: 461 PEACHSTONE TERRACE SAN RAFAEL CA 94903
8/20/2012	ANSWER DEFT, KAYO KIMURA
8/20/2012	PAUPERIS FILING GRANTED DEFT, KAYO KIMURA
8/20/2012	ANSWER DEFT, FRANK THORNALLY
8/20/2012	PAUPERIS FILING GRANTED DEFT, FRANK THORNALLY
8/20/2012	ANSWER DEFT, ROY HOPPE
8/20/2012	PAUPERIS FILING GRANTED DEFT, ROY HOPPE
10/9/2012	CASE REMOVED AS CONFIDENTIAL
10/9/2012	PAST 60 DAY LIMIT
12/31/2012	MINUTE ORDER POSTED - Appearance: 12/31/2012 at 08:30 AM for OSC RE: DISMISSAL JUDGE/PROTEM/REFEREE ROY O. CHERNUS , REPORTER NOT REPORTED , DEP CLK D.THAI NO APPEARANCE BY OR FOR THE PARTIES

MARIN SUPERIOR COURT OF CALIFORNIA, COUNTY OF MARIN		
ANK OF AMERICA, N.A. Plaintiff(s) VS. AMUEL H. SLOAN, ET. AL. Defendant(s)	DATE FILED:	8/8/2012
	CASE TYPE:	Civil Complaint
	CASE SUBTYPE:	Unlawful Detainer
	DATE OF LAST ACTIVITY:	12/31/2012
	DATE/TIME RUN:	1/28/2013 12:02pm
REGISTER OF ACTIONS	CASE NUMBER:	CIV 1203665

IT IS ORDERED:

CASE DISPOSED BEFORE TRIAL; DISMISSED - OTHER REASONS WITHOUT PREJUDICE

CASE DISPOSED IN ENTIRETY

ENTERED BY: D.THAI

MARIN SUPERIOR COURT OF CALIFORNIA, COUNTY OF MARIN		
BANK OF AMERICA, N.A. Plaintiff(s) VS. SAMUEL H. SLOAN, ET AL Defendant(s)	DATE FILED:	10/9/2012
	CASE TYPE:	Civil Complaint
	CASE SUBTYPE:	Unlawful Detainer
	DATE OF LAST ACTIVITY:	12/10/2012
	DATE/TIME RUN:	1/28/2013 12:02pm
REGISTER OF ACTIONS	CASE NUMBER:	CIV 1204541

INVOLVED PERSON/PARTY AND ATTORNEY SUMMARY:

BANK OF AMERICA, N.A. is the Plaintiff and is represented by: ROTHSTEIN, GARY D.; URBACH, MATTHEW S.

SLOAN, SAMUEL H. is the Defendant and is represented by: PRO PER

HOPPE, ROY is the Defendant and is represented by: PRO PER

THORNALLY, FRANK is the Defendant and is represented by: PRO PER

KIMURA, KAYO is the Defendant and is represented by:

REGISTER OF ACTIONS:

10/9/2012	CASE OPEN / ACTIVE STATUS Hon. Roy O. Chernus
10/9/2012	NOTICE OF RERLATED CASE: CIV 1203665 BANK OF AMERICA, N.A., AS TRUSTEE VS SLOAN; HOPPE; THORNALLY; KIMURA; AND DOES 1 - 10
10/9/2012	CASE MARKED AS CONFIDENTIAL
10/9/2012	FILING FEE PROCESSED: PLTF, BANK OF AMERICA, N.A. - 240.00
10/9/2012	COMPLAINT/FIRST PAPER DOES NOT EXCEED $10,000
10/9/2012	SUMMONS ISSUED AND FILED
10/9/2012	FULL NAME PLTF: BANK OF AMERICA, N.A., TRUSTEE OF THE TRUST FOR MICHAEL CREATED UNDER THE GOODALL TRUST DATED 9/12/1990
10/9/2012	HEARING CONFIRMED FOR: 03/05/2013 AT: 08:30 AM FOR APPEARANCE TYPE: OSCH IN DEPARTMENT: D06
10/9/2012	HEARING CONFIRMED FOR: 04/09/2013 AT: 09:00 AM FOR APPEARANCE TYPE: CSCM IN DEPARTMENT: Z7
10/19/2012	UD PROPERTY LOCATION: 461 PEACHSTONE TERR SAN RAFAEL CA 94903
10/19/2012	ANSWER DEFT, SAMUEL SLOAN
10/19/2012	FILING FEE PROCESSED: DEFT, SAMUEL SLOAN - 225.00
10/19/2012	ANSWER DEFT, FRANK THORNALLY
10/19/2012	PAUPERIS FILING GRANTED DEFT, FRANK THORNALLY
10/22/2012	ANSWER DEFT, ROY HOPPE
10/22/2012	PAUPERIS FILING GRANTED DEFT, ROY HOPPE
10/22/2012	ANSWER DEFT, KAYO KIMURA
10/22/2012	PAUPERIS FILING GRANTED DEFT, KAYO KIMURA
10/23/2012	PROOF OF SERVICE FILED, AS TO: DEFT, KAYO KIMURA; BY PERSONAL SERVICE ON 10/10/12
10/23/2012	PROOF OF SERVICE FILED, AS TO: DEFT, SAMUEL H. SLOAN; BY PERSONAL SERVICE ON 10/10/12
10/23/2012	PROOF OF SERVICE TO ALL UNNAMED OCCPANTS; BY SERVING SAMUEL H. SLOAN AND POSTING ON 10/11/12
10/24/2012	PROOF OF SERVICE FILED, AS TO: DEFT, ROY HOPPE; BY SUBSTITUTED SERVICE ON KAYO KIMURA, CO-OCCUPANT ON 10-11-12 AND BY MAIL ON 10-12-12.

MARIN SUPERIOR COURT OF CALIFORNIA, COUNTY OF MARIN		
BANK OF AMERICA, N.A. Plaintiff(s) VS. SAMUEL H. SLOAN, ET AL Defendant(s)	DATE FILED:	10/9/2012
	CASE TYPE:	Civil Complaint
	CASE SUBTYPE:	Unlawful Detainer
	DATE OF LAST ACTIVITY:	12/10/2012
	DATE/TIME RUN:	1/28/2013 12:02pm
REGISTER OF ACTIONS	CASE NUMBER:	CIV 1204541

4/2012 PROOF OF SERVICE FILED, AS TO: DEFT, FRANK THORNALLY; BY SUBSTITUTED SERVICE ON 10-11-12 ON KAYO KIMURA, CO-OCCUPANT AND BY MAIL ON 10-12-12.

1/2012 APPEARANCE ADDED ON FOR: 11/28/2012 AT: 08:30 AM FOR APPEARANCE TYPE: LMCV IN DEPARTMENT: D06

8/2012 MINUTE ORDER POSTED - Appearance: 11/28/2012 at 08:30 AM for MOTION FOR SUMMARY JUDGMENT

JUDGE/PROTEM/REFEREE ROY O. CHERNUS , REPORTER PRIVATE CONTRACT REPORTEER, JO DILLINGHAM BREWER, CSR 9707 , DEP CLK S. DIENER

ATTORNEY EUGENE L. HAHN APPEARED FOR PLAINTIFF

DEFENDANT/RESPONDENT ROY HOPPE IS PRESENT IN PRO PER

DEFENDANT/RESPONDENT KAY KIMURA IS PRESENT IN PRO PER

DEFENDANT/RESPONDENT FRANK THORNALLY IS PRESENT IN PRO PER

DEFENDANT/RESPONDENT SAMUEL SLOAN AS ADMINISTRATOR OF THE GOODALL TRUST AND IS PRESENT IN PRO PER

MOTION(S) HEARD AND ARGUED.

THE TENTATIVE RULING IS AFFIRMED AND MADE FINAL.

********* EXCEPT OF RULING, SEE COURT'S FILE FOR COMPLETE RULING ***********

MOTIONS FOR SUMMARY JUDGMENT BY PLAINTIFF BANK OF AMERICA, N.A., TRUSTEE OF THE TRUST FOR MICHAEL CREATED UNDER THE GOODALL TRUST DATED SEPTEMBER 21, 1990, AGAINST DEFENDANTS SAMUEL SLOAN, ROY HOPPE, FRANK THORNALLY, AND KAY KIMURA ARE DENIED.

HEARING BEFORE TRIAL

ENTERED BY. P. OKUBO

0/2012 CASE REMOVED AS CONFIDENTIAL

MARIN COUNTY SUPERIOR COURT
3501 Civic Center Drive, Room 113
P.O. Box 4988
San Rafael, CA 94913-4988

PLAINTIFF:
Bank of America N.A.
vs.
DEFENDANT:
Samuel H. Sloan Et Al

CASE NO. CIV 1203665

CIVIL MINUTES
ORDER TO SHOW CAUSE
Dismissal

CSCRT **JUDGE** Roy O. Chernus **DATE/TIME** 12-31-12 / 830 **CLERK** DT
APATT **ATTORNEY** ____ **appeared for** ____
APPPP **Plaintiff/Petitioner** ____ **is present in pro per.**
APNAP **No appearance by or for the parties.**
APNAB **No appearance by or for the** ____
CSMDT **THE COURT MODIFIES MANDATORY APPEARANCE DATES ON CASE MANAGEMENT SCHEDULE AS FOLLOWS: PREVIOUS DATES VACATED.**

Filing of Proof of Service ___/___/___ 8:30 / 9:00 a.m.
Filing of Answer or Default ___/___/___ 8:30 / 9:00 a.m.
Case Management Conference ___/___/___ 8:30 / 9:00 a.m.

APOSC **ORDER TO SHOW CAUSE ISSUED FOR:**
(Name): ____
For Failing to Appear on ___/___/___ or file ☐ Proof of Service ☐ Request to Enter Default
As to ____

YOU ARE HEREBY ORDERED TO APPEAR IN COURT AS SET FORTH BELOW TO SHOW CAUSE WHY YOU FAILED TO COMPLY WITH THE STANDARD FILING REQUIREMENTS OF THE CASE MANAGEMENT SCHEDULE IN THE ABOVE REFERENCED CASE:
Date: ___/___/___ 8:30 / 9:00 a.m. Courtroom: ____ before Judge: ____

☐ FNSMS ☐ **SANCTIONS ARE TO BE PAID BY** ____ **TO THE MARIN COUNTY SUPERIOR COURT IN THE SUM OF $** ____ **BY** ___/___/___ **FOR:** ____

☐ CSTXT ____

☐ CSDLP **Case dismissed, lack of prosecution**
☒ CSDOT **Case disposed before trial; Dismissed, other reasons** Without prejudice
☒ CSDSP **Case disposed in its entirety**

Pltf to serve minute order

Roy O. Chernus
JUDGE OF THE SUPERIOR COURT

DECLARATION OF PERSONAL SERVICE/SERVICE BY MAIL
(Code of Civil Procedure Sections 1013a and 2015.5)

I, the undersigned, under penalty of perjury, declare that I am over 18 years of age, a citizen of the United States, an employee of the County of Marin and not a party to the action. I served this *Civil Minutes Order* by ☐ Personal Service, or ☒ Service by Mail (by placing true copies thereof, enclosed in a separate envelope, with postage fully prepaid by the filing party, in the United States Post Office mail box, at San Rafael, Marin County, California) on the date written herein, addressed to the parties/counsel as indicated on the complaint.

Zaler Lopez
11355 West Olympic Blvd
Los Angeles, CA 90064

Gary Rothstein
One Embarcadero Center 30th
San Francisco, CA 94111

Executed at San Rafael, California
1 / 2 / 13

KIM TURNER
Court Executive Officer
By: DTZ

Exhibit G

Marin County Superior Court Unlawful Detainer Proceedings Case Numbers Civ 1204541 tentative ruling adopted as final ruling denying motion for summary judgment

SUPERIOR COURT OF CALIFORNIA
COUNTY OF MARIN

DATE: 11/28/12 TIME: 8:30 A.M. DEPT: B CASE NO: CV1204541

PRESIDING: HON. ROY O. CHERNUS

REPORTER: Jo Dillinham Brewer, CSR 9707 CLERK: ~~DUONG THAI~~ S. Dillon

PLAINTIFF: BANK OF AMERICA, N.A.	EUGENE L. HAHN (π)
vs.	ROY HOPPE, Δ PRO PER KAYO KIMURA, Δ PRO PER
DEFENDANT: SAMUEL H. SLOAN, ET AL	FRANK THORNALLY, Δ PRO PER SAMUEL SLOAN, Δ PRO PER AND ADMINISTRATOR OF THO GOODALL

NATURE OF PROCEEDINGS: 1) MOTION FOR SUMMARY JUDGMENT – AGAINST SLOAN AND KIMURA [PLTF] BANK OF AMERICA, N.A.
2) MOTION FOR SUMMARY JUDGMENT – AGAINST DEFTS HOPPE AND THORNALLY [PLTF] BANK OF AMERICA, N.A.

ARGUED

RULING ADOPTED

Motions for Summary Judgment by Plaintiff Bank of America , N. A., Trustee of the Trust for Michael created under the Goodall Trust dated September 12, 1990, against defendants Samuel Sloan, Roy Hoppe, Frank Thornally, and Kayo Kimura are denied.

As against Sam Sloan and Kayo Kimura, plaintiff seeks judgment for possession based on orders of the San Francisco Superior Court and the July 27, 2012, Sixty-day notice. Plaintiff has put its title to the property "at issue" in this unlawful detainer proceeding. The bulk of the allegations in the Complaint and the "Undisputed Facts" in support of the subject motion for summary judgment are addressed to plaintiff's extensive efforts by way of collateral proceedings in San Francisco Superior Court to confirm that the premises is an asset of the Trust for Michael created under the Goodall Trust dated September 12, 1990, that title to the premises is in Bank of America as trustee, and that plaintiff may administer the premises pursuant to the terms of Trust. Yet despite plaintiff's extensive allegations detailing the San Francisco proceedings, plaintiff does not actually allege or demonstrate via undisputed facts that the orders of the SF Sup. Ct. are "final" or that the issue of its title to the subject property has been fully and finally determined. Plaintiff appears to base its right to commence this unlawful detainer proceeding upon the **Minute Order** of the SF Superior Court dated July 19, 2012, denying defendant's petition for reconsideration as plaintiff served the subject 60-Day Notice eight days later on July 27, 2012, ***even though the court's order was not formally entered until September 27, 2012.*** (See Complaint, ¶19, and Exh. E.) Even *assuming* the order denying defendant's petition for reconsideration constitutes a final and binding determination of plaintiff's title (though not specifically alleged), plaintiff served the 60-day notice before that Order was formally entered on September 27, 2012. This unlawful detainer action was filed a mere 12-days later on October 9,

2012. As stated by the Court in *Greenhut v. Wooden* (1982) 129 Cal.App.3d 64, 68, "this is not your usual garden variety type of unlawful detainer action" where the issue of title is strictly limited. Having put its own title in issue and by relying on the San Francisco Trust proceeding as the source of its authority to commence this proceeding, plaintiff should demonstrate that title to the property has, in fact, been finally adjudicated in its favor. Plaintiff's pleading and evidence falls short of demonstrating a final adjudication of title in its favor and raises a question of fact whether the alleged 60-day notice was served prematurely.

As to defendants Hoppe and Thornally, a complaint for unlawful detainer must allege that the tenant continues in possession of the premises. (CCP §1161.) No cause of action for unlawful detainer exists if the tenant has quit before the action is filed. Defendants Hoppe and Thornally have filed answers admitting they have relinquished possession of the premises. In its motion, plaintiff claims that while Hoppe and Thornally have relinquished physical possession of the premises, "plaintiff is informed that Hoppe and Thornally have not relinquished their alleged *right* to possession of the premises." If a landlord wishes to determine *rights* to possession, but not physical possession, it cannot do so by way of summary unlawful detainer; a quiet title action would be the proper remedy.

In the event that no party requests oral argument in accordance with Marin County Superior Court Local Rules, Rule 1.6 B., the prevailing party shall prepare an order consistent with the announced ruling as required by Marin County Superior Court Local Rules, Rule 1.7.

Exhibit H

San Francisco Probate Court Transcript of Hearing dated July 19, 2012 In Re The Goodall Trust

SUPERIOR COURT OF THE STATE OF CALIFORNIA

COUNTY OF SAN FRANCISCO

In the Matter of the Trust for Michael created under the Goodall Trust dated September 12, 1990.
______________________________/

CASE NO. PTR-99-273030

BEFORE HONORABLE JUDGE PETER J. BUSCH

TRANSCRIPT OF PROCEEDINGS
____

July 19, 2012

2:00 p.m.

San Francisco Superior Court
400 McAllister Street, Room 204
San Francisco, CA 94102

REPORTED BY: NOEL CARTER DEGNAN, CSR No. 6921

WEST COAST REPORTERS
177 Paul Drive, Suite A
San Rafael, CA 94903
(415) 472-2361 * (800) 979-2361
FAX (415) 472-2371
email: depos@westcoastreporters.com

A P P E A R A N C E S

FOR THE PETITIONER SAM SLOAN:

LAW OFFICES OF SAM WARE
By: SAM WARE, Attorney at Law
700 Larkspur Landing Circle, Suite 199
Larkspur, CA 94939
Phone: (415) 464-4872

FOR THE PETITIONER BANK OF AMERICA:

MANATT, PHELPS & PHILLIPS, LLP
By: GARY D. ROTHSTEIN, Attorney at Law
One Embarcadero Center, 30th Floor
San Francisco, CA 94111
Phone: (415) 291-7400

FOR THE OBJECTOR GUIDE DOGS FOR THE BLIND:

REED SMITH, LLP
By: ALICIA ADORNATO, Attorney at Law
1999 Harrison Street, Suite 2400
Oakland, CA 94612
Phone: (510) 763-2000

Thursday, July 19, 2012 2:00 p.m.

P R O C E E D I N G S

THE BAILIFF: All rise. Court is now in session. The Honorable Judge Peter J. Busch presiding. Please be seated.

THE COURT: Thank you. Good afternoon.

MR. WARE: Good afternoon, Your Honor.

MR. ROTHSTEIN: Good afternoon, Your Honor.

THE CLERK: This is case number 273030, In Re: The Goodall Trust.

MR. WARE: Sam Ware appearing on behalf of Sam Sloan, the Administrator of the Estate of Michael Goodall.

MR. ROTHSTEIN: Gary Rothstein appearing on behalf of Trustee Bank of America.

MS. ADORNATO: Alicia Adornato appearing on behalf of Guide Dogs For The Blind.

THE COURT: Could you spell your last name?

MS. ADORNATO: A-d-o-r-n-a-t-o.

THE COURT: Thank you.

MR. WARE: And the record will also reflect that Mr. Sloan is here.

THE COURT: All right. This is Mr. Sloan's motion for reconsideration, and as you know my tentative ruling is to deny it. I don't think that there are new or different facts or circumstances within the meaning of the statute, and in any event there's nothing in there that leads me to change my views.

MR. WARE: Your Honor, thank you very much for the opportunity to be heard on this matter. The first matter that I would like or first issue I would like to address is a jurisdictional one and here is I guess my concern.

In the declaration of Mr. Sloan which we filed in support of the motion Mr. Sloan declares that these documents which we have attached to his declaration were not discovered earlier because they were locked up in a locked cabinet. And so I don't know -- excuse me, please.

THE CLERK: Please make sure all your electronic devices are turned off.

MR. WARE: Sorry for the interruption, Your Honor. So if there are any questions, Mr. Sloan has traveled out here yesterday from New York to address any concerns that the court might have as to his delay or the explanation for the delay in discovering these documents. If there are, he is here to address any of those concerns by whomever, the parties or the court. So that's the first point or offer I'd like to make with regard to the jurisdiction.

The second thing I'd like to point out is that Mr. Sloan upon discovering these documents felt duty bound to bring them to the attention of the court and to make them part of the record.

Your Honor, the significance of those documents is that, with regard to the document attached as Exhibit A to Mr. Sloan's declaration, it is a heretofore undiscovered document which is a Power of Attorney where Rachel Goodall appoints her son Michael Goodall as her attorney in fact should her husband Kenneth Goodall not survive, and we know that he did not, and that appointment was endorsed by Kenneth Goodall in that document.

The significance of that, Your Honor, in our view is that it goes to the intent of the Goodalls. What we have in the 1994 amendment, Your Honor, was an amendment which went from trust to trust and which was a bit circuitous as the court will recall. In fact, that's the reason that Bank of America came to court and asked for clarification, and the court found based upon the record at the time at the last hearing it was the intent -- reading that document, that it seemed to be the intent of the Goodalls to give the rest of the estate to Guide Dogs For The Blind.

The other bit of evidence on intent was the declaration of Hastings where he said that he remembered that the Goodalls told him that he had no -- they didn't trust Michael with the money and so they wanted to put anything that he would get into a trust.

The document which we have attached as Exhibit A and which was discovered in this locked cabinet speaks to that issue of intent, Your Honor, and we wanted to bring that to the court's attention less we be forever barred from making that part of the record. So that was our submission there.

With regard to the second document which we described, which is a document also discovered in this locked cabinet and also wanted to make part of the record, Your Honor, is a document which is a Power of Attorney, Michael Goodall's Power of Attorney which demonstrates -- which is evidence that, as I was urged in the court last time, that Mr. Hastings here had a conflict of interest, that he was serving several masters at the same time and that that conflict of interest ought to be considered when the court is trying to determine whether or not the authenticity of the operative document here, the 1994 amendment, should be considered.

So those are the documents that we've asked the court to consider and with those documents to reconsider its earlier ruling.

Now, I want to speak a minute, please, to the issue of the it-really-doesn't-matter argument, whether that document -- whether the 1994 amendment is authentic or not doesn't matter, because any claims made by Mr. Sam Sloan as Administrator of the Estate of Michael Goodall are no better than the claims of Michael Goodall and Michael Goodall went beyond his rights of 120 days and therefore would be barred from making these arguments, challenging the authenticity of the 1994 trust, et cetera.

I will just reiterate the point that reasonable minds may differ as to the sufficiency of the notice, whether it needs to identify in words with one syllable that the document being noticed to Mr. Michael Goodall was the 1994 amendment as well as the 1990 trust which was specifically identified in the notice.

But there's another point, Your Honor, which in reviewing this matter I want to bring to the court's attention. Perhaps it has been considered, though I have urged this today, that although the notice here, this Probate Code Section 116061.7 notice was drafted and signed by Mr. Hastings in July of 1999, it was not served until October of 1999. And as we know, this action was filed within 120 days of the service of that notice. This action was filed in I believe it was December of 1999.

So we have the notice that was dated in July, apparently was served in October, so October, November, December, it's 60 days. January certainly this case was alive. It had been filed. So the concept or the principle which is applicable to the Statute of Limitations defense here is that in addition the relation back argument.

Observation here, Your Honor, that this action has been pending, Statute of Limitations have been tolled on anything related to the facts which underlie the petition which was described in the petition first filed in December for a very long time, but they're still alive.

So with that, Your Honor, I submit it. I thank you for your time. I understand the court's tentative ruling. I understand I have an appeal fight here, but I do want to make sure that the record is complete for the benefit of my client and for the benefit of his beneficiaries. Thank you very much.

THE COURT: Thank you, Mr. Ware. Mr. Rothstein?

MR. ROTHSTEIN: Thank you, Your Honor.

With respect to the notification that was served under Probate Code 16061.7, perhaps that was served October 1999 and perhaps Michael Goodall filed an initial petition here in this proceeding in December of 1999. That proceeding was nothing more than a declaratory relief petition to ask the court to confirm that if in fact he filed a petition subsequently to remove the bank as trustee, which he did, that this would not be a contest under the -- of the 1994 restatement.

The 120-day Statute of Limitations is a bar to an action by which the beneficiary would be challenged and the validity of the trust. Michael never did that. To the contrary. He made it very -- he very carefully acted with independent counsel, by the way, not Mr. Hastings as his counsel, he acted very carefully to make sure he was not challenging the validity of the trust because he knew the consequences if he did. So the Statute of Limitations absolutely applies in this matter and bars anything, any action by Mr. Sloan at this point to challenge the validity of the trust on behalf of Michael.

Therefore, any documents that have been supposedly located in some locked cabinet at this point are completely irrelevant. This court has already ruled. The Statute of Limitations applies, and Mr. Ware has really argued nothing new in that regard. Thank you, Your Honor.

THE COURT: Okay. Do you have anything?

MS. ADORNATO: I would underscore what Mr. Rothstein just said. These are all matters that were discussed the last time we were here. There's nothing new that has been presented. I would just agree with everything Mr. Rothstein said on that point.

THE COURT: The tentative ruling will stand. Did you have a Form of Order?

MR. ROTHSTEIN: No, Your Honor.
MS. ADORNATO: No, Your Honor.
MR. WARE: No, Your Honor.
THE COURT: I'm going to ask Mr. Rothstein to prepare a Form of Order denying you the motion. It's perhaps indicated through the silence on the tentative ruling. The court is not going to impose sanctions at this time.
MR. WARE: Thank you, Your Honor.
MR. ROTHSTEIN: Thank you, Your Honor.
THE REPORTER: Mr. Rothstein, would you like to order a copy of this transcript?
MR. ROTHSTEIN: No, thank you.
THE REPORTER: Mr. Ware, would you like to order a copy of the transcript?
MR. SLOAN: Yes, I would.
MR. WARE: Okay. That's the answer.
(Proceedings adjourned at 2:15 p.m.)

CERTIFICATE OF REPORTER

I, NOEL CARTER DEGNAN, CSR 6921, duly authorized to administer oaths pursuant to Section 2093(b) of the California Code of Civil Procedure, hereby certify that the foregoing proceeding was reported by me and thereafter transcribed by me or under my direction into typewriting.

I further certify that I am not of counsel nor attorney for either or any of the parties in the foregoing proceeding and caption named, or in any way interested in the outcome of the cause named in said caption.

____

NOEL CARTER DEGNAN, CSR#6921

Exhibit I

San Francisco Probate Court Transcript of Hearing dated September 20, 2012 In Re The Goodall Trust

SUPERIOR COURT OF THE STATE OF CALIFORNIA

COUNTY OF SAN FRANCISCO

BEFORE HONORABLE JUDGE PETER J. BUSCH

In the Matter of the

Trust for Michael Goodall created under the Goodall Trust dated September 12, 1990. /

CASE NO. PTR-99-273030

TRANSCRIPT OF PROCEEDINGS

September 20, 2012

2:30 p.m.

San Francisco Superior Court
400 McAllister Street, Room 204
San Francisco, CA 94102

REPORTED BY: NOEL CARTER DEGNAN, CSR No. 6921

WEST COAST REPORTERS
177 Paul Drive, Suite A
San Rafael, CA 94903
(415) 472-2361 * (800) 979-2361
FAX (415) 472-2371

APPEARANCES

FOR THE PETITIONER SAM SLOAN:

LAW OFFICES OF SAM WARE
By: SAM WARE, Attorney at Law
700 Larkspur Landing Circle, Suite 199
Larkspur, CA 94939
Phone: (415) 464-4872

FOR THE PETITIONER BANK OF AMERICA:

MANATT, PHELPS & PHILLIPS, LLP
By: EUGENE L. HAHM, Attorney at Law
One Embarcadero Center, 30th Floor
San Francisco, CA 94111
Phone: (415) 291-7400

ALSO PRESENT:

SAM SLOAN

Wednesday, September 20, 2012 2:30 p.m.

P R O C E E D I N G S

THE BAILIFF: All rise. Court is now in session. The Honorable Judge Peter J. Busch presiding. Please be seated and come to order.

THE CLERK: Hi, Judge. This is case number 273030, the Goodall Trust.

THE COURT: Thank you. Good afternoon.

MR. WARE: Good afternoon, Your Honor.

MR. HAHM: Good afternoon, Your Honor.

THE COURT: Appearances.

MR. HAHM: Eugene Hahm with Manatt, Phelps & Phillips appearing on behalf of the trustee Bank of America.

THE COURT: Good afternoon.

MR. WARE: Sam Ware appearing at this time on behalf of Mr. Sloan and myself.

THE COURT: Good afternoon.

MR. WARE: Good afternoon. Thank you.

MR. SLOAN: And I'm Sam Sloan. I don't know if I have to appear or not.

THE COURT: As I indicated in my tentative ruling, the first question is whether to grant the request for a continuance here. I guess my question, Mr. Ware, is what would be gained by that? What is it that you couldn't present this afternoon that somehow you could later?

MR. WARE: Your Honor, I have not been in this circumstance in my career. I have given it a lot of thought and I have spoken with the ethics hotline at the Bar. For reasons which I would be comfortable talking to Your Honor in camera at the time of the motion to withdraw, I believe that I cannot say anything on behalf of either myself or Mr. Sloan with regard to this motion until -- with regard to the sanctions motion until the motion to withdraw is heard and at that time be given the opportunity as requested in my moving papers to speak to the court in camera about my circumstances. But until that happens, Your Honor, I'm afraid I feel quite tethered and I would ask for the court's understanding and grant the motion to continue.

THE COURT: Mr. Hahm?

MR. HAHM: Your Honor, as we indicated in our reply papers, we do object to any continuance. We filed this motion basically two months ago. We stipulated to a continuance at Mr. Ware's request to accommodate his vacation schedule. Before he went on vacation he did file a provisional opposition. Mr. Sloan filed an opposition. Mr. Ware still had time to file an opposition to be timely for this hearing. I don't see any basis obviously for a furtherance, and we feel that we've been put to a lot of prejudice in opposing a motion that should not have been brought. And quite frankly, this request for a continuance could have been raised a long time ago when we first served our sanctions motion back in June.

THE COURT: Well, the problem is none of us know, with the exception of Mr. Ware and maybe Mr. Sloan at this point, what precipitated the motion and when and how it affects this. That's the problem that I'm facing here is I don't know that any of that is right. And Mr. Ware has told me as an officer of the court that he has information that is pertinent but that he is ethically prevented from providing at this time.

MR. HAHM: Well, the difficulty I have, Your Honor, respectfully, is that the subject of the sanctions motion is very limited. It was the propriety of the motion for reconsideration that was filed back in May when Mr. Ware was counsel. He filed that motion under his own pleading papers and signed it, and he gave an accounting for the reasons for doing so after we had served him with the sanctions motion, that he was essentially acceding to the wishes of his client.

Now, if there's some back story there, that may be all well and good, but Section 128.7 imposes an obligation on a lawyer not to file frivolous pleadings with the court just because your client says so, and there are remedies for that. You can withdraw as counsel at that point in time. You can continue the hearing on the motion for reconsideration so that you could go ahead and seek a voluntary withdrawal or substitution. What you don't do is proceed with the motion, disregard the sanctions brief that we served, challenge the tentative and proceed as if everything is copacetic.

The bank has filed this motion and did it with tremendous consideration. We know that sanctions are serious motions. Your Honor knows better than anyone else about the reasons for having the rules for motions for reconsideration, and we just think that they were violated here and there wasn't enough seriousness or consciousness put into the filing. Especially after we put them on notice that this was sanctionable behavior.

THE COURT: Mr. Ware, anything else?

MR. WARE: Your Honor, what I would say is that there was activity during the so-called safe-over period which I again would be able to discuss with the court in camera but not at this time. And I am asking again, please, for the court's understanding and continue the matter until after the motion to withdraw is heard and I can present this information to the court again.

THE COURT: Just as a note, to the extent that

you intend to present information responsive not to the motion to withdraw but to the pending motion for sanctions, I do not anticipate taking that in chambers.

To the extent that there are things that you would think that you still -- that were pertinent to the pending -- to this motion that's before us today that you would want to present in some confidential way, I don't think you're going to have that opportunity.

MR. WARE: No. The point, Your Honor -- I understand the court's observations and caution. My point is this, Your Honor. That I would like to have the opportunity to file a further opposition to the motion for sanctions, but by -- but the content of that and the preparation of that opposition requires that I first know whether the court will allow me to withdraw because I would be in a different position, Your Honor, after that motion is heard with regard to the opposition, which I intend to file. I do not intend to keep any secrets in that regard, but I need to be -- I need to extricate myself from my present representation preliminarily according to my understanding of my pickle at this point ethically.

THE COURT: Okay.

MR. HAHM: May I respond, Your Honor?

THE COURT: Yes.

MR. HAHM: I will keep this short. Two thoughts. One is I'm sort of in a guessing game here because I'm assuming that Mr. Ware intends to file something in a further opposition that might be provisionally subject to some kind of attorney-client privilege. I don't see that that privilege would be waived unless it was done so voluntarily by Mr. Sloan, and I'm also assuming that he wouldn't do so right now, otherwise he would have stipulated to Mr. Ware's withdrawal from representation.

Time is an issue for the bank. One thing that's not presently before Your Honor is what's going on with the occupancy of the house in Marin. There is an unlawful detainer proceeding because, as I understand it, Mr. Sloan continues to occupy these premises even though based on Your Honor's order this is real property that belongs to the beneficiary of the trust.

THE COURT: None of that turns on this motion.

MR. HAHM: No. But there is a certain -- there is a nexus in that we are trying to proceed with these unlawful detainer proceedings, Your Honor, and as long as Mr. Sloan is here fighting the UD, I know I'll have an opportunity to enforce potentially sanction motions if Your Honor were to award any sanctions. If this gets kicked down the road a little bit farther, I don't know what the likelihood would be of our being able to enforce that.

MR. WARE: May I ask one more thing? I beg your pardon. One thing that I have not yet seen come in the court is an order on the motion for reconsideration, and it's my understanding that it was submitted by counsel for Bank of America months ago. I would just inquire as to the status of that.

MR. HAHM: Your Honor, if I may, I think that's correct. I believe that an inquiry had been made to the examiner from my office maybe a couple of weeks ago just on the status, but I don't think it's been formally signed. I believe all parties have approved the Form of Order.

THE COURT: Do you have a copy of it?

MR. HAHM: I don't. I apologize. I can have it resubmitted certainly.

THE COURT: Do you have the date of the motion?

MR. HAHM: The motion for reconsideration, yes, I do.

MR. WARE: July 19th I believe.

MR. HAHM: July 19th. That's correct.

THE CLERK: I do not see an order in here.

THE COURT: I don't have any sitting on my desk. So I don't know what's become of it. So why don't you resubmit it.

MR. HAHM: Certainly, Your Honor.

THE COURT: If you resubmit it to the clerk's attention, that might be the best most effective way of making sure it gets to my desk.

MR. HAHM: I'll do that, Your Honor. I'll do it today.

THE COURT: And if it's been approved as to form, then it will get signed and out.

I'm going to grant the continuance. I don't know either whether there are appropriate things that will be able to be said that can't be now, but the only information I have is what Mr. Ware has told me. I don't want to inquire now into the issues concerning the motion to withdraw because that isn't before me and I don't want to put Mr. Ware in a position where he either has to violate his ethical obligations or cannot properly defend himself from what is a serious motion. Even if there -- even, Mr. Hahm, if your analysis is correct and what Mr. Ware may have to say couldn't exonerate him from sanctions, it may still affect the amount of sanctions. May affect the conditions under which the court would or wouldn't choose under its discretion to award sanctions. I just don't know and I don't want to guess. I don't think it's appropriate. So I'm going to grant a continuance. The motion is set for October 30th?

MR. WARE: Correct.

THE COURT: What I would ask Mr. Ware is that you have your supplemental opposition ready to go so that if the court does grant your motion at that time it can then be promptly filed and we're not looking at a new period of time to allow for its preparation.

MR. WARE: I understand.

MR. HAHM: Your Honor, can we set up a specific briefing schedule and hearing date?

THE COURT: We're going to set a new hearing date. October 30th is the hearing on that motion. Let me ask this first. Is there any objection to advancing the hearing date to October 29th by one day so that I'll be available to hear it?

MR. WARE: Fine for me.

THE COURT: Mr. Sloan, do you have any objection?

MR. SLOAN: It's all right with me.

THE COURT: Mr. Hahm, any problem with that?

MR. HAHM: No, Your Honor.

THE COURT: Not that you have much of a role in that motion.

MR. HAHM: As far as I know, I don't intend to appear at that hearing, and I don't believe Guide Dogs has any objection to Mr. Ware's motion on it.

THE COURT: All right. So I am going to advance

the October 30th hearing to October 29th. Let's specially set it for 10:30.

MR. WARE: Fine. Thank you.

THE COURT: So we can get out of the traffic of the regular Monday morning hearing a little bit.

With that said, I would then like to continue this hearing. If there is to be any supplemental opposition filed by Mr. Ware, it will need to be filed by November 1st.

MR. WARE: Thank you.

THE COURT: And then we would have -- well, you're going to want an opportunity to reply to that?

MR. HAHM: I'd like to reserve that opportunity, Your Honor.

THE COURT: That supplemental reply, if it is to be filed, will need to be filed by November 7th and we'll set a hearing date of November 15th if we have room.

THE CLERK: We do.

MR. WARE: 15th, Your Honor?

THE COURT: Yes.

MR. WARE: Time 2:30?

THE COURT: November 15th. It can be 2:00 o'clock. 2:00 o'clock November 15th.

MR. WARE: May I ask one more thing, Your Honor, at this point? Should Mr. Sloan wish to file anything further, what would be the appropriate time for that?

THE COURT: Mr. Sloan has filed something now. Mr. Sloan has no such ethical problems. I'm not sure why Mr. Sloan would be entitled to any subsequent filing on this motion. Obviously, Mr. Sloan will be able to respond to your motion to withdraw, but on this motion I'm not sure why there would be an opportunity. If Mr. Sloan thinks that he has that right, anything that he would file would have to be filed by November 1st, but that would be subject to a request to strike it I suppose.

MR. HAHM: For the record, Your Honor, we did object.

THE COURT: Actually, let me back away from that for just a second. Mr. Hahm, you have objected to his filing what he's filed?

MR. HAHM: Correct.

THE COURT: And once he is no longer represented by Mr. Ware in this matter, he would certainly have the right to file something.

MR. HAHM: The continuance, as I understand it though, Your Honor, is to afford Mr. Ware the opportunity to provide further briefing on the reasons for his conduct. Mr. Sloan has filed a very fulsome opposition which we objected to because it was --

THE COURT: Right. If the court were to sustain

that objection, then he would have nothing on file and that can't be right. You can either withdraw the request to strike that or I'm going to have to give Mr. Sloan an opportunity as well to file his own opposition if it turns out that he is no longer represented by Mr. Ware. That's your choice.

MR. HAHM: I suppose, Your Honor, what I will do is I will -- can I withdraw my objection if the court grants the motion?

THE COURT: No, because I don't want that hanging out there because I don't want to then have to delay this hearing again to allow Mr. Ware an opportunity to -- I don't want to force him to prepare something looking into that uncertainty.

MR. HAHM: Mr. Sloan?

THE COURT: Mr. Sloan.

MR. HAHM: That's fine, Your Honor. If Mr. Sloan ends up representing himself, then we will reserve the right to respond to any supplemental reply that he may file. May I ask one clarification? And that is if he gets new counsel in the meantime or if after withdrawal of Mr. Ware is granted if he retains new counsel as part of that process, does he then get another bite of this apple?

THE COURT: I don't know. I don't know.

Mr. Sloan, if you intend to file anything else

with respect to this motion, it will also be due by November 1st. Okay?

MR. SLOAN: All right.

THE COURT: All right. Thank you all.

THE REPORTER: Counsel, would you like to order a copy of the transcript?

MR. HAHM: Let me check with my colleague. I have your card.

MR. SLOAN: We want it. Don't worry.

MR. WARE: They'll deal with me. I'll make sure you get it right away. Yes. That's probably easiest. Thank you.

(Whereupon, the proceedings were adjourned at 2:56 p.m.)

CERTIFICATE OF REPORTER

I, NOEL CARTER DEGNAN, CSR 6921, duly authorized to administer oaths pursuant to Section 2093(b) of the California Code of Civil Procedure, hereby certify that the foregoing proceeding was reported by me and thereafter transcribed by me or under my direction into typewriting.

I further certify that I am not of counsel nor attorney for either or any of the parties in the foregoing proceeding and caption named, or in any way interested in the outcome of the cause named in said caption.

____

NOEL CARTER DEGNAN, CSR NO 6921

Exhibit J

San Francisco Probate Court Transcript of Hearing dated October 29, 2012 In Re The Goodall Trust

SUPERIOR COURT OF CALIFORNIA

COUNTY OF SAN FRANCISCO

In the Matter of the   CASE NO. PTR--99--273030

Trust for Michael created
under the Goodall Trust dated
September 12, 1990.

_________________________________/

BEFORE THE HONORABLE PETER J. BUSCH

REPORTER'S TRANSCRIPT OF PROCEEDINGS

October 29, 2012

10:36 a.m.

San Francisco Superior Court
400 McAllister Street, Department 204
San Francisco, CA 94102

REPORTED BY: ADRIENNE MEDA, CSR NO. 6609

-o0o-

A P P E A R A N C E S

For the Petitioner Sam Sloan:

LAW OFFICES OF SAM WARE
Sam Ware, Attorney at Law
700 Larkspur Landing Circle, Suite 199
Larkspur, CA 94939
(415) 464-4872

Also present:

Arden Van Upp

Monday, October 29, 2012 10:36 a.m.

P R O C E E D I N G S

THE COURT: Thank you. Good morning.

MR. WARE: Good morning, Your Honor.

THE CLERK: This is line 47, case number 273030, The Goodall Trust.

MR. WARE: Sam Ware. Good morning, Your Honor.

MR. SLOAN: Good morning, Your Honor. I'm Sam Sloan.

THE COURT: Good morning.

All right. The request has been that this matter go forward in camera. Therefore, the Court is prepared to close the courtroom for that purpose.

THE CLERK: Which I have already locked the doors, Your Honor.

THE COURT: There is somebody else here.

MR. WARE: It's a friend of Mr. Sloan's who will listen, and I have no objections.

THE COURT: Okay.

Mr. Sloan, you understand that her presence here may mean that there is no privilege with respect to things which are said in the courtroom?

MR. SLOAN: I'm waiving all privileges, anyway.

THE COURT: All right. That's fine. The matter is being recorded. The transcript of this proceeding is to be under seal and not to be released to anyone other than the parties present today without further order of the Court. Unless you're waiving that?

MR. SLOAN: I'm waiving that.

THE COURT: That's fine. Then it need not be under seal.

All right. I have the pending motion for Mr. Ware to be relieved with the request that he be permitted to further -- to tell the Court further information about it. So what we're going to do is, I'll hear from Mr. Ware, and then I'll hear anything Mr. Sloan would like to say, and proceed from there, assuming, Mr. Sloan, that you're opposing that?

MR. SLOAN: Yes, Your Honor. Actually, I would even like to testify, if possible.

THE COURT: Well, we're not going to have testimony, but you'll be permitted to make the arguments you want.

MR. WARE: Thank you. Your Honor, I didn't know that the motion was being opposed. I have received no written opposition to describe what that opposition may be. I would, however, address the Probate examiner's notes, which she, Ms. Trowbridge, I believe it is, who kindly sent me her notes describing that, in her review of the papers, there had been no declaration in support of a motion. Your Honor, with all due respect to Ms. Trowbridge, I did file the form declaration.

THE COURT: Her point was not that you didn't file the necessary form, her point was that it doesn't tell us anything about why you think it's appropriate for the Court to allow you to withdraw, which is your opportunity to do now.

MR. WARE: Thank you.

The reason that I want to withdraw, Your Honor, is that I believe that there is a personality conflict between Mr. Sloan and I, and a fundamental difference as to how to approach this case. And the -- and I did provide a declaration with that general statement in my declaration in support of attorney's motion to be relieved as counsel. And that was under penalty of perjury. I followed that general declaration as suggested, as the suggested format in all of the referenced materials, which I reviewed in preparing this motion. The advice being that to say as little as possible with regard to the grounds for the motion to withdraw, until it's opposed, and then I've asked at that point any in camera disclosed in more detail the reasons that I feel that that's appropriate relief at this time.

The first thing I would say, Your Honor, is and I would like the opportunity to address any opposition, because I don't know what that is.

THE COURT: You'll find out in a minute. But first I need to know what the basis for the request is. And then Mr. Sloan will have more to tell us, more basis to present whatever his opposition is. So let's go forward. Go ahead.

MR. WARE: The reason that I want to get out, Your Honor, is that for the second time now, Mr. Sloan has filed papers without even consulting me in this case. Months ago, a hearing was held by Judge Dearman, where there had been an opposition to the motion to distribute or to confirm the beneficiaries. And I regret that I don't have that exact paper in here, but I asked at that point that the paper had been filed that I had no idea was happening. And I asked Judge Dearman to give me a leave to amend that so as to remove some of the vituperative that was contained in that. And Judge Dearman kindly granted me to leave to amend that.

Here an opposition to the motion for sanctions, again a long -- and a long opposition was filed, Your Honor, that I just had no forewarning of, or wasn't consulted about. And I just can't -- I can't have it. I can't live like that. I can't practice law like that. This has never happened to me before. I just can't endorse a lot of what was said in there, and so I've got to get out.

And I've asked Mr. Sloan to let me out, to sign a stipulation or substitution of attorneys and, he hasn't returned it, for what reason, I don't know. And Mr. Sloan and I just have a basic disagreement and have had a disagreement as to this motion for sanctions.

I, quite frankly, I want to get out of it. When I got the papers from Bank of America that threatened sanctions, I thought, you know, I think it was probably a good opportunity to avoid the sanctions issue, and I recommended that we, Mr. Sloan, withdraw the motion, and we had disagreement on that. And so not wanting to abandon Mr. Sloan, we went forward on that. But, you know, Mr. Sloan has kindly agreed that I can talk about that and appreciate that.

But he was very insistent that this thing go forward, this motion for reconsideration. But, you know, I think that's defensible within the realm of reasonable minds can differ as to the liability for that motion for reconsideration, and I will file a further opposition describing that. But the fact of the matter is that we disagree, disagreed, and things are being filed without my approval and consultation. I simply can't practice law like that.

THE COURT: Okay. Mr. Sloan?

MR. SLOAN: I have quite a -- lots of things and will probably leave out most of them because I have a lot to remember, but in the first place, as far as the two documents --

THE COURT: You need to slow down a little bit.

MR. SLOAN: I'll try to slow down. I do have a bad habit of talking fast. It's hard to break it.

As far as the two documents I filed, Mr. Ware has told me that he was on trial and in jury trial, I believe it was in Hayward. He would not be able to come back for about 10 days. He was out of town, and he asked me to file opposition to this motion which is coming up in a few days, otherwise, it would be too late to file it. And I have the letter that he wrote asking me to file a motion.

What he's really complaining about is that I said that based on the new documents that we had discovered, I am certain, 100 percent certain, that the trust document is a forgery. And the reason I'm certain of that is because we now have a document dated the same date, filed by the same people with the same Notary Public August 24th, 1994, and comparing the two documents, the trust document also dated August 24th, 1994 signed by all the same people, it is obvious that the signatures are so much different that they could not possibly be signed by the same person. It is utterly impossible that the same people signed these two documents at the same time on the same date. Out of the question.

And since Bank of America refuses to produce their document, they only sent us a fax 14 years later, 2008 faxed document, they refused to produce the original document. And we have lots of other documents signed by these people with consistent signatures of this type and a completely different document.

It is clearly a forgery. Mr. Ware doesn't want me to say that is a forgery because he feels he'll get in trouble with the bar and the courts by accusing opposing counsel of using a forged document to win a court case, but that is our case. Our case is that it is a forgery.

Mr. Ware has known that this is our case from the very beginning, although we didn't discover these documents until quite recently, until after you had actually made a decision on the case.

So now Mr. Ware wrote me a letter -- which I have in my pocket but I don't need to produce it because it more or less repeats what he just said -- which is that he wants to withdraw as counsel because they have filed a motion for sanctions against me and against him, and they want $16,000 in attorney's fees, and that motion is now pending, which will be heard I think November 15th.

So he's saying that, if he can get off this case, then he can get out from under the motion for sanctions. But we've known from the beginning when he took this case on a contingency-fee basis. I think in general he has done an excellent job. I think he's really done the best job that he could do. I'm certainly not complaining about him. Although, I do think that he was unwilling to bring up these issues of the forgery, the improperization (Sic.), the Notary signatures were not valid, done in a proper Notary Public form, lots of other -- the fact that they refused to produce the documents, the fact that we subpoenaed all the documents, didn't produce a single document, all these things, irregularities in the case, he has been not very aggressive in asserting these points. So I think -- and he's a rather mild mannered, polite person, that's his style -- and I think that it has been for the most part successful -- but he didn't start this motion to withdraw until after you had already issued I think a final decision in this case, and then they filed their motion for sanctions.

And what he's trying to do is trying to get away from the motion for sanctions by withdrawing from the case. And I don't think that's the proper way to do it. He should fight the motion. And I don't think that also even served his purpose. I don't think that by withdrawing from the case, he defeats the motion for sanctions anyway. I'm not sure one thing is related to the other.

So, basically, I think that the Court can't just give him leave to withdraw just because his really only reason is to defeat the motion for sanctions.

Oh, yes, the second thing was the two documents I filed. Number one was when he was out of town, he was out of town for about 10 days in a jury trial. He couldn't get it done. He asked me to do it. But then he said oh, well, I put this other -- some other word documents, copies of exhibits and things like that which he had not presented to the Court, so I added more things to it.

But, as I said, Judge Dearman granted leave to amend, and he did amend, and, in fact, he basically kept the same basic points as I was making in the document I filed, he more or less repeated them in a more or less more polite way.

The second time was, again, the hearing was coming up in three days, he was away on vacation for nearly a month. And I had to file something because, otherwise, it was no opposition to his motion. It turns out he got an extension of time and didn't come back. Well, he came back two weeks later. There was enough time, but at that particular time I think the date was -- I can't remember the exact date, but I think it was August 30th, something like that. And if something didn't get filed, we were going to be on default. So I had to file something. And he told me to file something because he was coming back. I have the letter he wrote me -- actually, it's on the email asking me to file something to make sure we didn't go on default on this motion because he was out of town. And opposing side was not agreeing at that point to postpone the hearing on that.

So -- and again, because he's actually making this motion to withdraw after the Court has already issued a judgment in this case, it's a little bit late to suddenly want to withdraw from the case. And especially since he took the case on a contingency basis, he knew this was a big case involving about a two and a half million dollars estate, and that they were prepared to fight dirty in order to win this case. We've known that from the get-go they'll do anything. Because what we think really happened, is we think they've actually spent the two and a half million dollars, and they can't get it back, so they'll actually lose the whole money if we win the case. And we think that's what is really happening. Otherwise, why would they care about this case. Supposedly they are going to donate to a charity. Why would they care so much.

They have nine attorneys on this case. Nine attorneys opposing us all together. And they are making a tremendous effort on a case which supposedly they are just a stake holder and have no stake in the outcome. That is a very strange thing with why is B of A fighting this case so hard when they claim to have nothing at stake in this case, maybe a matter of principal.

And, of course, they've never even given any grounds. They have not produced a single document. Not even one document. No grounds have been given for the case. No cases have been sited. They filed the same motions that they filed in this court. They filed exactly the same motions in Marin County Probate Court, which appointed me the administrator.

I don't think they should have been allowed to file this lawsuit in this court when I'm acting under the orders of the Marin County Probate Court. I don't think you should even be hearing this case at all right now. You should dismiss this case, because it's a Marin County case, has nothing to do with San Francisco. This case has no connection with San Francisco at all. No reason for this case even to be before you. And I don't know why you would entertain this case when it's clearly inappropriate for this case, when the property is a Marin County estate, is in Marin County, buried in Marin County, had nothing do at all -- didn't even like to come to San Francisco. Why is it the case of these people and I'm representing -- I'm the person representing these people, appointed by the Court. Why is Bank of America allowed to file a case here when the case belongs in Marin?

So that basically in summary is why I'm opposing his motion to withdraw. And, like I say, it's too late. You've already made a judgment in this case. I don't even think you have jurisdiction to entertain this case, as a matter of fact, at this point.

THE COURT: Okay. Mr. Ware, anything else?

MR. WARE: I would just make these observations, Your Honor, that the record of the court will show that I have dutifully challenged the authenticity of the amendment, but I would not go so far as to accuse people of forgery. That's true. And the Court, with regard to these two filings without my approval or signature, again, the record -- the fact is that with regard to the first document, I did ask Mr. Sloan to file the document that I had prepared, but what was filed, in fact, was more than I had prepared. There were additional content added to that document and which I did not have the opportunity or was not asked for input to file.

So with regard to the second document, the most recent opposition to the motion for sanctions which was filed by Mr. Sloan, I just have nothing to do with that, and I had absolutely nothing to do with instructing Mr. Sloan to file anything in that regard. It simply was done.

And I would say, finally, that -- I have nothing more, actually. I have nothing more.

Submitted, Your Honor. I think that the record does demonstrate the grounds that I have summarily described in my declaration. We just simply have a difference of conflicting personalities here on this matter, and we simply can't in unity approach anything on this case any further.

MR. SLOAN: I have one more thing to say about this, about the second document. The motion for sanctions was not -- see, I represent the Estate of Michael Goodall. But the motion for sanctions was for $16,000 in attorney's fees against me and Mr. Ware personally. If this is granted, we are both personally liable for the $16,000. So, therefore, at that point, I'm not in my capacity as the court-appointed administrator to the estate, it's in my personal capacity that they are asking for $16,000.

And, secondly, the estate at this point doesn't have any money anyway, so I'm going to have to pay out of my own pocket. So, therefore, I do have the right and obligation to defend myself. And I made it quite clear in the papers, if you read them, it says Mr. Ware is out of town, I haven't had a chance to talk to him, I'm filing this opposition because I need to -- because I need to defend myself against this motion for $16,000 in attorney's fees. And the motion -- if you look at the motion, it's directed at me personally, not just at the Estate of Michael Goodall, which I'm the personal representative of. So I think I had the right, and Mr. Ware was away on vacation for almost a month, so that's why I had to do something. I couldn't just simply let their thing go into default.

THE COURT: Okay. Submitted?

MR. WARE: Submitted.

THE COURT: All right. The motion is going to be granted. I think that Mr. Ware has made it clear that there is a breakdown in the attorney-client relationship that requires the Court to allow him to withdraw at this time. Most of what Mr. Sloan is -- has argued simply isn't relevant to that question, and to the extent that what he's argued is shows that there are different interpretations of some of the events but doesn't fundamentally rebut what I think is the necessary finding here; that Court cannot require Mr. Ware to continue to represent Mr. Sloan under these circumstances. That's going to be the Court's order.

Do you have a form of order?

MR. WARE: I have a form of order. I haven't shown it to Mr. Sloan, but I believe --

THE COURT: It needs to be on the Judicial Counsel form for withdrawal.

MR. WARE: Yeah. Thank you. I'll do that.

THE COURT: So you can submit that form of order, make sure that it correctly states the current future dates. I think you had a proposed order which did not. And the Court will be in the position to sign that.

MR. WARE: I'll consult the forms. Thank you. Sorry for that oversight.

MR. SLOAN: Can I keep that?

MR. WARE: You can keep that, of course.
Thank you very much.
THE COURT: All right. Thank you.
MR. WARE: Thank you.
(Off the record.)
(The proceedings adjourned at 10:57 p.m.)
-o0o-

SUPERIOR COURT OF THE STATE OF CALIFORNIA

COUNTY OF MARIN

I, ADRIENNE MEDA, do hereby certify that: the proceedings in the foregoing hearing were duly reported by me in the within-entitled cause; that said hearing was taken at the time and place as set forth; that the said proceedings was reported by me, a Certified Shorthand Reporter and a disinterested person, and was thereafter transcribed by computer under my direction into booklet form.

I further certify that I am not of counsel or attorney for either or any of the parties in the foregoing proceeding and caption named, nor in any way interested in the outcome of the cause named in said caption.

Executed November 20, 2012, 2012, at San Rafael, California.

Adrienne Meda, CSR No. 6609

Exhibit K

San Francisco Probate Court Transcript of Hearing dated November 15, 2012 In Re The Goodall Trust

SUPERIOR COURT OF CALIFORNIA
COUNTY OF SAN FRANCISCO

In the Matter of the CASE NO. PTR--99-273030

Trust for Michael created under the Goodall Trust dated September 12, 1990.

______________________________/

BEFORE THE HONORABLE PETER J. BUSCH

REPORTER'S TRANSCRIPT OF PROCEEDINGS

November 15, 2012

2:09 p.m.

San Francisco Superior Court
400 McAllister Street, Department 204
San Francisco, CA 94102

REPORTED BY: ADRIENNE MEDA, CSR NO. 6609

-o0o-

APPEARANCES

In Pro Persona:

SAM H. SLOAN

LAW OFFICES OF SAM WARE
Sam Ware, Attorney at Law
700 Larkspur Landing Circle, Suite 199
Larkspur, CA 94939
(415) 464-4872

For the Trustee, Bank of America:

MANATT, PHELPS & PHILLIPS, LLP
Eugene L Hahm
1841 Page Mill Road, Suite 200
Palo Alto, CA 94304
(650) 812-1377

Also present:

Arden Van Upp

Thursday, November 15, 2012 2:09 p.m.

P R O C E E D I N G S

THE COURT: Thank you. Good afternoon, everyone.

THE CLERK: This is case number 273030, The Goodall Trust.

THE COURT: Appearances?

MR. HAHM: Good afternoon, Your Honor. I am Eugene Hahn, appearing on behalf of Trustee, Bank of America.

MR. WARE: Sam Ware responding -- one of the responding parties.

MR. SLOAN: I'm Sam Sloan, the other responding party. I'm here Pro se because the Court signed an order removing my attorney as counsel, so now I'm on my own.

THE COURT: We have before us this afternoon Bank of America's motion for sanctions based on the filing of the motion for reconsideration, which the Court has denied. I'm going to hear argument this afternoon on that issue and that issue only on the basis of the papers which have been properly filed, which does not include Mr. Sloan's filing of yesterday, which was untimely and not provided for and not allowed by the Court.

And on relevant argument that's presented

today, Mr. Hahn?
MR. HAHM: Thank you, Your Honor. It's obviously my queue, since I have contested the tentative. And I'm going to be brief, because most of the points that I've wanted to make have been in our papers. I'll make two brief points.
The first is that I think it's very clear that the purported new evidence that Mr. Sloan discovered after the hearing on the motion for reconsideration just did not qualify as new evidence under section 1008 of the Code of Civil Procedure. And section 1008 also is very explicit that sanctions can be awarded for a litigant's failure to observe the requirements of 1008.
So this is a case where I believe the motion for reconsideration should never have been filed. I believe that the new evidence was not germane to the legal issue that will form the basis of the Court's underlying ruling on the original petition for instructions.
So the motion for reconsideration shouldn't have been filed, but, at minimum, it should have been withdrawn once we served our sanctions motion. And I can confide to the Court that we thought long and hard about filing that motion because it's often cost ineffective.

You spend a lot of time, and then the offending pleading can be withdrawn voluntarily. But we thought it was an appropriate measure given some of the rhetoric that had gone back and forth in this case, mostly slung by Mr. Sloan directly.

Unfortunately, that motion for reconsideration was not withdrawn, and as a result, we, Bank of America, myself, we had to go to additional expense in preparing an opposition to the motion for reconsideration and then ultimately appearing at the hearing, which, as Your Honor noted, you denied that motion for reconsideration. So it generated additional unnecessary expense for the Trustee.

And that brings me to the second point, which is, I think it's very clear from the totality of the circumstances that there may have been some improper motive in pursuing -- in Mr. Sloan's pursuing this motion for reconsideration in the first place. The Court alluded to it somewhat in the tentative ruling, but as you look at all the filings, it's clear that Mr. Sloan wanted to use the motion for reconsideration as a platform for him to be able to re-argue the same things that he had argued in the underling motion, which was in the 1994 trust amended was a forgery that Jim Hastings was a crook, and that Bank of America and Guide Dogs For the Blind were all part of this conspiracy. And this is the level that we've been seeing from Mr. Sloan.

I understand the Court has not considered or is not considering the papers that he filed yesterday, but his original opposition that was filed in August accused not only Bank of America and Jim Hastings and Guide Dogs of corrupt behavior, but he accused all the attorneys associated in this case, Gary Rothstein, of lying to the Court and called this Court as making bone-headed decisions and suggesting that the reason why Guide Dogs was getting away with murder was that this Court was corrupt.

I understand the Court's tentative. I do believe that sanctions are appropriate here, certainly with respect to Mr. Sloan, and the Court has discretion to allocate sanctions in that matter because the record suggests that that motion, along with many other filings in this case, was presented primarily for harassment purposes. And that's certainly something that you get when you call out attorneys and trustees and threaten them with sanctions or disbarment. And we have a situation where one of the litigants here will say virtually anything and stop at nothing to be able to make that point.

I presented in our supplemental reply some

email correspondence from Mr. Sloan indicating that he was going to start a scorched earth campaign against Guide Dogs. He has also, stated by his own admission, circulated over 4,000 mailers about this litigation and the corruption of Guide Dogs and also stated in those mailers that the reason we can get away with this is that the courts are in our pockets.

I don't represent Guide Dogs, I represent Bank of America, but this is the level of inductive that we're seeing, and I believe, if only for the principle, some award of sanctions should be applicable against Mr. Sloan for his involvement for filing this motion for reconsideration.

THE COURT: Thank you, Mr. Hahm.

Which of the respondents would like to --

MR. WARE: Submitted, Your Honor.

MR. SLOAN: Your Honor, okay, first place is you said you didn't read my filing of yesterday. However --

THE COURT: I didn't say I didn't read it, I said I'm not going to consider it because it was improper.

MR. SLOAN: But on the 7th of November, Bank of America filed two declarations, and mine was -- essentially was in response to their two declarations.

Their filing was improper.

THE COURT: So, sir, you were in court when we set this hearing, and at that time, you and Mr. Ware were permitted to file supplemental oppositions on November 1st, and then the Bank of America was permitted to file a supplemental by November 7th. That all happened. The thing that was improper was your filing yesterday.

MR. SLOAN: Your Honor, okay, the next thing is if -- since you didn't read the filing --

THE COURT: I didn't say -- sir -- sir. You have a tendency in these filings, not to your benefit, to make misstatements repeatedly about things you cannot possibly know about, most particularly this Court's conduct.

I did not say I did not read it. I said I am not going to consider it in deciding this motion.

Go ahead.

MR. SLOAN: Okay. But this case was filed in Marin County Probate Court in January of 2011. It was filed in that court in January of 2011. I was appointed -- as a probate matter, I was appointed as the -- as the representative -- personal representative of the Goodall Trust.

THE COURT: No, you were appointed as

personal representative of the Goodall Estate.

MR. SLOAN: Goodall Estate.

THE COURT: Very different thing, which you seem not to appreciate.

Let me stop you for just a second. My tentative ruling was to deny this motion for sanctions, and I explained in part why that was. I've heard from Mr. Hahm. Mr. Hahm doesn't change my mind at the moment. I'm going to listen to whatever it is you want to say. You need to understand that, first of all, as I indicated, I think you've shown, in part at least, your motives in the motion were improper and that ultimately what was presented the Court didn't find relevant. However, I concluded that sanctions were not proper.

If you wish to make a presentation now, of course, the only thing that can happen is that I might reconsider that.

MR. SLOAN: Well, Your Honor, I haven't been able to speak this whole time, because Mr. Ware was my attorney. Just a few minutes ago, you signed an order withdrawing him as my attorney. So up until now I've not been allowed to speak in this case. My point is -- is that their motion on the basis of statute of limitations which made that motion in March within County Probate Court, they filed that motion there. There was a hearing on that motion, it was denied by Ms. Judge Verna Adams, so having that motion denied by Judge Verna Adams in that court, which is the proper court and that is where jurisdiction lies in this case because all the parties involved are Marin County people, they turned around and filed the same motion here.

THE COURT: And how can any of this be relevant to a motion to reconsider as opposed to the Marin Court's original decision, which is not at issue either in the motion to reconsider or today?

MR. SLOAN: I'm getting to that, Your Honor.

THE COURT: Okay.

MR. SLOAN: The document which they filed, which is the whole basis for their motion, it was not timely filed. They only filed it five days before the hearing date. It was a document, which I have in my hand, which we've never seen before. We had subpoenaed all of their documents. They had not produced a single document, and in particular they have not produced this three-page letter. This three-page letter doesn't contain any letterhead, doesn't contain any information about who's writing the letter, and since we have subpoenaed all their documents, and they didn't produce the documents, and they only filed this thing five days before the hearing date before you, it was just they were pulling a rabbit out of the hat. They were coming up with some completely new theory that had never been introduced before. And it's based on a letter supposedly to Mike Goodall giving him 120 days to respond, but we don't know whether he responded or not because he never produced the file in this case.

We subpoenaed the file, we made motions here. Mr. -- the motion for a hearing was actually a discovery motion saying we want to see the documents. You haven't produced any documents on this case. So we had every right to file that thing.

And, secondly, as I've pointed out, the Bank of America broke into the house and burgled the house, stealing the entire contents of the house, and they put it over McCann's Auction House, which they were trying to sell at auction.

THE COURT: All of which happened before the original hearing. Correct --

MR. SLOAN: Because --

THE COURT: -- therefore, it was not a proper subject for a petition for re-hearing, which is the only issue before the Court, whether there was a proper basis for that motion, and if not, whether the Court should issue sanctions on the basis of that motion.

MR. SLOAN: But they filed a motion -- they

didn't give us enough time to respond. That was the whole point to the motion for re-hearing. They filed new documents.

THE COURT: That wasn't the point at all to the motion of re-hearing. But go ahead.

MR. SLOAN: Yes, it was in his papers that we could not respond to that motion because he filed it only five days before the hearing date, and we simply didn't have the opportunity to respond to that. That was one of the main points.

And, secondly, all these documents, which they stole from the house -- we were able to get them back and in storage boxes -- and eventually we found these documents which they have -- they created the documents. The documents which we called newly-discovered evidence were documents created by Bank of America, by their attorneys. So they had the documents from the beginning. And we found these documents after the motion for re-hearing, and we felt we had an obligation to the estate and the trust and people involved in this case -- a lot of people, not just me -- to present those documents to the Court. That's why we had to come back and present these documents which we had never seen before. If we had seen them before, we would have produced them because they were very much in our favor. But we didn't have the documents. The reason; Bank of America stole the documents, because they broke into the house. And we had to file an 850 motion before Judge Verna Adams in Marin County Probate Court. And eventually there was a hearing before Commissioner Goldfine in which they ordered either to return the documents or come to court and explain why. And eventually they chose to give the documents back. And that's how we got into our present situation.

So we didn't have a chance to explain that to you because we were short of time. By the way, I'm representing Pro se in Marin County Court, Mr. Ware does not represent me in Marin County for the simple reason I always win up there, so why should I pay him to be up there. I'm winning the case anyway. I hired him to represent me because we were losing the case down here, and we needed representation.

There's no grounds for sanctions against me or Mr. Ware. Certainly not Mr. Ware, because he's just carrying out my instructions and doing what I tell him to do.

THE COURT: Okay. Anything else, Mr. Hahm?

MR. HAHM: No, Your Honor. I submit.

THE COURT: Okay. All right. I am going to deny the motion. I am, it's indicated in the tentative ruling, troubled by Mr. Sloan's conduct in bringing a motion for reconsideration. I think the basis for it was very slim and that primarily it was intended to re-argue matters that had already been presented and decided. But I think that there was, and clearly had, at least in part, the additional improper motive of spreading irrelevant and improper allegations that had no business in the matter before the Court on the court record.

However, as I indicated in the tentative, I think there is enough there that, under the circumstances, sanctions at this stage would not be appropriate given the Court's discretion under section 1008 and section 128.7 to which it refers. So that is going to be the Court's ruling.

Did you have a form of order?

MR. WARE: Not yet, Your Honor. I'll prepare an order.

THE COURT: I would appreciate that.

MR. HAHM: Thank you, Your Honor.

THE COURT: Thank you.

(Off the record.)

(The proceedings adjourned at 2:24 p.m.)

-o0o-

SUPERIOR COURT OF THE STATE OF CALIFORNIA

COUNTY OF MARIN

I, ADRIENNE MEDA, do hereby certify that: the proceedings in the foregoing hearing were duly reported by me in the within-entitled cause; that said hearing was taken at the time and place as set forth; that the said proceedings was reported by me, a Certified Shorthand Reporter and a disinterested person, and was thereafter transcribed by computer under my direction into booklet form.

I further certify that I am not of counsel or attorney for either or any of the parties in the foregoing proceeding and caption named, nor in any way interested in the outcome of the cause named in said caption.

Executed November 27, 2012, 2012, at San Rafael, California.

Adrienne Meda, CSR No. 6609

Exhibit L

Marin County Superior Court Transcript of Hearing dated November 28, 2012 in Bank of America vs. Samuel H. Sloan, et al Case No. CIV 1204541

SUPERIOR COURT OF CALIFORNIA

COUNTY OF MARIN

Bank of America, N.A., Trustee of the Trust for Michael created under the Goodall Trust dated September 12, 1990

CASE NO. CIV 1204541

Plaintiff,

vs.

SAMUEL H. SLOAN, an individual; ROY HOPPE, an individual; FRANK THORNALLY, an individual; KAYO KIMURA, an individual; and DOES 1-10, inclusive,

Defendants.

_______________________________________/

REPORTER'S TRANSCRIPT OF PROCEEDINGS

HONORABLE ROY O. CHERNUS, JUDGE

DEPARTMENT B

NOVEMBER 28, 2012

REPORTED BY: JO DILLINGHAM BREWER, CSR NO. 9707

WEST COAST REPORTERS
117 Paul Drive, Suite A
San Rafael, CA 94903
(415) 472-2361 * 800-979-2361
Fax (415) 472-2371

A P P E A R A N C E S

For the Plaintiff:

EUGENE L. HAHM, ATTORNEY AT LAW
MANATT, PHELPS & PHILLIPS, LLP
One Embarcadero Center, 30th Floor
San Francisco, California 94111
(415) 291-7400

For the Defendant:

SAMUEL H. SLOAN, in Pro Per
461 Peachstone Terrace
San Rafael, California 94903
(415) 419-5980
(917) 659-3397

---oOo---

11/28/12 P R O C E E D I N G S 10:00 A.M.

THE COURT: Bank of America versus Samuel Sloan. May I have appearances for the record?

MR. SLOAN: Yeah, my name is Samuel H. Sloan, 461 Peachstone Terrace, San Rafael, California. I am the administrator with will annexed of the estate of K. Michael Goodall.

MS. KIMURA: My name is Kayo Kimura. I'm living in the estate of -- the house at -- living with him and my daughter.

THE COURT: Thank you.

MR. THORNALLY: I'm the defendant Frank Thornally. I do not live in the house. I've been out of the house for a couple of years. But, anyway, I'm named in this, so here I am.

THE COURT: Thank you.

MR. HOPPE: My name is Roy Hoppe. Similar to Frank, I moved into a homeless shelter two years ago because of Mr. Hastings' threats. And I have not lived in the house for -- since the end of January of 2011, I believe, it is. I've been gone for two years.

THE COURT: Thank you.

MR. HAHM: Good morning, your Honor. I am Eugene Hahm with Manatt, Phillips, appearing on behalf of the plaintiff, Bank of America, trustee of the Goodall

Trust.

THE COURT: Okay. I assume that it's the plaintiff that wants to contest my tentative ruling.

MR. HAHM: Yes, your Honor. Thank you.

There were four of the motions for summary judgment brought against the four defendants. I think I'd like to start, at the outset, with the summary judgment rulings with respect to Mr. Sloan and Ms. Kimura. And we did review the tentative ruling very carefully, and I think there may have been some confusion created by our carriers, and I apologize for that. But I'm here to go ahead and set the record straight and explain to the Court why there are no triable issues of fact that are suitable for an unlawful detainer trial, why we have met all the elements that we need to as summary judgment plaintiff in a unlawful detainer suit, and why judgment should be entered, first, against Mr. Sloan and then Ms. Kimura.

Now, Mr. Sloan filed an opposition, I believe, on Monday, to the motion for summary judgment. And as you can see, if you had the opportunity to review it, it's very extensive. He wants to convert what should be a summary expeditious unlawful detainer proceeding into a full-blown evidentiary hearing on a trust challenge. He wants to introduce evidence about Kenneth and Rachel

Goodall's testamentary intent, whether a document that they had signed 20 years ago was forged, whether there was corruption in the courts, whether there was some type of fraudulent behavior brought by Bank of America's former counsel some years ago, Jim Hastings. And all of that is going to be improper, your Honor, and I will address that in a moment.

So let me go ahead and start with what is in the record and is utterly undisputed. And that is, first, Bank of America, as the trustee of the Goodall Trust, properly served a 60-day notice to terminate upon all the defendants back in late July. Undisputed. Sixty days has expired. They had not vacated the premises. And we have not accepted any rent after the expiration of that 60-day notice. Under any other circumstance, this would be a garden-variety UD action, and judgment would be warranted on a summary judgment. That's what undisputed.

THE COURT: Except that the San Francisco Superior Court confirmed that the premises was an asset of the trust until September 27th.

MR. HAHM: And let me go ahead and address that.

So, number one, Mr. Sloan and, I believe, Ms. Kimura, in their answers to the UD complaint, asserted affirmative defenses that Bank of America was an improper plaintiff. So two points. Number one, as a general rule, questions about title are not proper for adjudication in unlawful detainer proceedings. I have two citations for that that weren't in our papers. One is Drybread v. Chipain Chiropractic 151 Cal.App.4th 1063 and High v. Cavanaugh 205 Cal.App.2d 495. Again, they state the proposition that issues about title of the property are not proper defenses in a UD action. So that's number one, just as a legal matter.

Number two, there's a statement in the tentative ruling, which I'll go ahead and read, that says or suggests that "the plaintiff is relying on the San Francisco trust proceeding as a source of its authority to commence this proceeding."

And, your Honor, I respectfully say that that's an incorrect statement. We are not relying on the probate proceedings as the authority to commence this proceeding. And I apologize for any confusion that may have been created by our papers. I want to be very, very clear. Bank of America, as the trustee of the Goodall Trust, its position that it is the proper plaintiff because the property has been an asset of the Goodall Trust since 1990 at least. Over 20 years. We did not need any further approval from the Probate Court in San

Francisco in order to commence this proceeding. The evidence in the record demonstrates that the house has been an asset of the Goodall Trust since the early '90s, and this is all set forth in the Declaration of Alex Bruner. I'll go ahead and summarize that very, very briefly because I think it's important and it will help dispel any sort of confusion that we may unintentionally have created.

So let's just go back a bit. The house was originally owned by Kenneth and Rachel. They were husband and wife. And, in 1990, they created the Goodall Trust. In connection with that, they both executed a quitclaim deed in favor of the Goodall Trust. In other words, the Goodall trust at that time became the title owner of that property. Bank of America was designated as the successor trustee of the Goodall Trust. Both Kenneth and Rachel were the initial trustees, and while they were alive they were going to serve in that capacity. Kenneth passed away in 1994 at which point Rachel became the sole trustee. Rachel passed away in 1999. At that point Bank of America became the trustee of the Goodall Trust of which the Peachstone Terrace residence was an asset. For that 13-year period -- or 12-year period, I should say, between 1999 and 2010 when their son Michael passed away, it was the Goodall Trust that clearly was the owner. If there had been any sort of accident that occurred, then the liable entity might have been that trust. The point is we have been serving in the capacity as trustee ever since that point in time. We don't need and did not need to file the Petition for Instructions in San Francisco Probate Court to commence this UD proceeding because we have the authority and the trust document itself, and we have been serving as landlord. That's number one.

Now, why did we go ahead and file that Petition for Instructions in San Francisco? And there are two. One instruction asks for the Court to confirm what we already knew, that the house was an asset of the trust as opposed to the estate of Michael Goodall; and then, two, to confirm what we believed to be true, that Guide Dogs for the Blind was the beneficiary of that trust. We referenced it in our papers because we reasonably anticipated that Mr. Sloan was going to raise this as an argument in his opposition to the summary judgment motion, that he was going to reassert that the Goodall Trust documents were all forged, that James Hastings was corrupt, should be disbarred, and that there is no basis for our pursuing this lawsuit. That's why we put it in there, just to explain that in a contested trust proceeding, all of his arguments had already been heard, had already been vetted and had already been adjudicated. That's what we wanted to convey to the Court. But we did not need it in order to commence this action. We are, on behalf of the Goodall Trust, the landlord, or the owner. And we are empowered to initiate an unlawful detainer action.

THE COURT: So it's just a coincidence that you filed -- that you served the 60-day notice within a few days after the minute order?

MR. HAHM: No, no. Absolutely. It was -- I don't want to call it "tactical." This was intentional. And let me go ahead and explain the reason behind filing the Petition for Instructions.

A trustee -- especially, a corporate trustee fiduciary like Bank of America tends to be very conservative. And this is what happened. After Michael Goodall passed away in 2010, Mr. Sloan opened a probate administration in Marin County Superior. And he indicated that the house was an asset of Michael Goodall's estate. We learned of that through my colleague, Gary Rothstein, who is mentioned repeatedly in his opposition papers. Had a discussion with Mr. Sloan, and we realized there was going to be some type of dispute. Therefore, we filed Petition for Instructions in San Francisco Superior, where the trust was being administered, to confirm what we knew to be true, what we believed to be true, which was the house is an asset of the trust. We do that to provide the trustee cover. Trustees do that all the time. And we got a ruling back in June of 2011 confirming -- confirming, not conferring -- but confirming that the house was an asset of the trust.

Jumping ahead a bit, I know that there's been no appeal of that. It's been well over 60 days -- obviously, June of 2011 -- and under California Rules of Court, it's 60 days of time that a litigant has a notice to file an appeal of an adverse ruling.

So getting back to your point, was it a coincidence? It wasn't a coincidence. We did it as a belt-and-suspenders approach. But we didn't have to. We could have proceeded just with our belts.

And the reason we did this, again, was we know that the opposition, Mr. Sloan, was going to reassert all of his arguments about the testamentary intent of the Goodalls, how the documents were falsified. And while we don't think any of those arguments are proper for an unlawful detainer proceeding, we wanted to go ahead and give the Court assurances that he had had his day in court, in other words; that he had had an opportunity to go ahead and explain to a court of competent jurisdiction about his arguments concerning the Goodall testamentary intent. And he has had that opportunity.

If the Court has any lingering concern about whether the authority to proceed with this lawsuit was conditioned upon the rulings in San Francisco Superior, I would suggest that that is an issue that is still a matter of law and not one that should be submitted to a trial. And perhaps supplemental briefing would be appropriate. It would be very short.

And the reason I say that is it's very, very, clear that this appeal that Mr. Sloan has filed from the two orders, one from June and one more recently, they're both entitled. And that's going to be clear from the First District. It's going to be rejected.

And we can brief that. It doesn't require any facts; it just requires request for judicial notice. But I don't think that's necessary. Because if this case is permitted to proceed, I'm not sure exactly what is going to be tried, whether Ken and Rachel Goodall actually signed documents 20 years ago, what the intent is. That's contrary to the purpose of UD, which is a summary of expeditious proceedings.

THE COURT: Thank you.

MR. SLOAN: Your Honor, this motion -- thank you for your tentative ruling, which I hope you accept.

This motion is certainly not amenable for summary judgment at all. Every single issue of fact is in dispute.

For one thing, the number one fact is the Bank of America, the trustee of the Goodall Trust, in the 1990 trust document -- and I've included the full trust document in my motion papers -- does not name the Bank of America successor trustee; it names Security Pacific Bank as the successor trustee.

Secondly, he doesn't mention that there was also a second amendment to the Goodall Trust dated January of 1990 -- of 1999, making Michael Goodall the successor trustee succeeding his father. So when his mother died, there were two trustees: Michael Goodall and his mother. They were the trustees of the Goodall Trust. And when Rachel Goodall died, then Michael Goodall, by right, became the sole trustee of the Goodall Trust. And because Bank of America insisted they were the trustee, he filed a case against them on December 21st -- 27th, 1999, against the Bank of America. And that case was still going in litigation for 10 years, until he died on October 5th, 2010. So all these issues that he's saying are undisputed issues are disputed issues. They have been disputed the whole time.

And, secondly, as far as his statement about

the documents, he has not yet -- we want discovery. They have not produced a single document since this case began. We have not seen that trust that he just said gives Bank of America -- makes them the trustee. They haven't produced that document. We want that document. We've made motions for that document, and we've served subpoenas for that document. We want depositions, especially of Hamilton Kipp and James Hastings. They won't agree to any discovery. The motion that they made was granted on a reply affidavit which they produced a document saying that Michael Goodall received something in the mail, but we didn't have even discovery to find out if he'd even answered it or if he really received it. So every single thing that he's talking about, these are things that are open to discovery and to issues of fact. I hope that you adopt the tentative ruling.

And by the way, I want to explain to Mr. Thornally and Mr. Hoppe, I'm the administrator of the estate. I was appointed by the probate judge here in Marin County. I don't know why they filed the case on the Goodall Trust in San Francisco when the proper venue and jurisdiction of this case was the same court, the same probate case that appointed me. They should not have been allowed to sue me in a different court than I was appointed from. I was appointed by the Marin County

Probate Court, and they should have brought this case in Marin County. Why they should -- they should never have been allowed to bring the case over in San Francisco when all the people died here, they are buried here, their wills are lodged here in the clerk's office in Room 113. You can look up the wills of the Goodall parents and their son. They never had anything to do with San Francisco. They never went there. They didn't even like to cross the Golden Gate Bridge. And because he feels that they couldn't -- we had three hearings in Probate Court. I would have prevailed in all three hearings. And that's why they went over to San Francisco three months later and got a case over there, because they realized that they couldn't win here.

So I'm hoping that you will adhere to the tentative ruling. I'm also hoping that you will order discovery that they have to produce the documents which they claim to be relying on.

THE COURT: I don't issue -- there's not a motion for -- to compel discovery, as I'm hearing. I'm just hearing the summary judgment motions.

Anything else, sir?

MR. SLOAN: I think they want to talk, too.

MS. KIMURA: Roy?

MR. HOPPE: Oh. I --

THE COURT: Actually, I think they already told me all that I need to know; that they're not living at the property.

MR. HOPPE: I'm not a legal maven, so I'm outside of my tent here.

THE COURT: Actually, you stated the most important thing; that both of you are not living at the property.

MR. HOPPE: Okay. I was the -- Mike's roommate for 13 years at that place. I was also his caretaker the last couple of years. I don't know if that's relevant to this case or not. I also know what Mike wanted.

THE COURT: Okay. That's not what I'm doing right now.

MR. HOPPE: Okay.

THE COURT: You're not in -- you're not living at the premises; is that correct?

MR. HOPPE: No.

THE COURT: And you're not living at the premises, either?

MR. THORNALLY: I am not living at the premises.

THE COURT: Okay. Thank you.

MR. HAHM: I'll make a couple of brief points,

your Honor. And then I didn't address the motion with respect to Mr. Hoppe and Mr. Thornally, and I'd like to address that very, very briefly.

First, Security Specific Bank became Bank of America back in 1991. We were the successor. You'll probably take judicial notice of it, but that was a very big transaction.

Number two, there was no form shopping when we initiated recently the Petition for Instructions in San Francisco Superior Court. We chose that venue because after Rachel Goodall died in 1999, Michael Goodall initiated a proceeding about the Goodall Trust in San Francisco. There was already a case opened there and, therefore, we filed our petition there.

In addition, ever since Rachel Goodall had passed away in 1999, Bank of America was the trustee of the Goodall Trust and had been operating under the assumption and belief that the house was an asset of that trust. So, again, if something had happened there, someone had been hurt, it wouldn't have been Michael Goodall who was responsible; it would have been the Goodall Trust. And as the trustee, Bank of America would be responsible for overseeing that. Bank of America, for example, would be the party that would initiate a quiet title action. If there was some sort of cloud on title

-- if there was a neighbor, for example, who alleged he had an easement over the backyard, well, it would be Bank of America, as the trustee of the Goodall Trust which has the title to the property, that would initiate that UD action. What happened in San Francisco in the probate proceedings wouldn't change what the title is; it just allowed us to proceed as if it were an asset of the Goodall Trust.

And everything Mr. Sloan has said about disputes concerning documents, discovery, amendments to the Trust, this has all been presented to San Francisco Superior Court twice -- multiple times, I should say, in the probate proceedings. There has been adjudications against him. They should be final, number one, because the time to appeal them has elapsed. And I'm happy to brief that. I can demonstrate to your Honor very clearly and --

THE COURT: Okay. You don't need to do that. And --

MR. HAHM: Okay.

THE COURT: -- I'm going to stop you there. I do believe that having argued about your right to bring this action and putting the title at issue, that even though it might have been a belt-and-suspenders approach, that you were then required to wait until the order from

San Francisco Superior Court was final. Now, what that means, according to my analysis, is if the bank gave a new 60-day notice, they would likely -- I would likely not find the same way on motion for summary judgment. I am going to stay with my tentative ruling though, in this case, as it's presently framed in front of me.

MR. HAHM: May I address one point with respect to Thornally and then Hoppe, your Honor?

THE COURT: Yes.

MR. HAHM: I understand that they don't have the premises. The concern that we had is if there exists those two gentlemen who were putative occupants and they weren't there, there would be no problem. But after the answer was filed on Mr. Hoppe, my colleague Mr. Burdock, spoke with him and asked him to stipulate that he's not going to reoccupy the premises, and he refused to stipulate.

MR. HOPPE: That's not true.

MR. HAHM: Well, in any event, at this point we have a complaint filed and an answer. The case is at issue. I suppose if they'll stipulate that they won't reoccupy, then I can dismiss against them. But I don't know what, procedurally, we're going to do. I can go to trial, or if the Court is dismissing it -- I'm in a bit of a bind right now.

THE COURT: Okay. Well, my tentative ruling is going to be the order of the court. And then I'm going to set this matter for trial. We're bound to have it tried fairly quickly, but you understand my notice -- finding -- what my likely finding is if we do a trial.

MR. HAHM: I understand, your Honor.

THE COURT: Why don't you think about that, and I will -- at this point I'm just going to stay my tentative ruling. That's all that's in front of me right now.

Thank you, all.

MR. HAHM: Do you need an order, or you do that?

THE COURT: Actually, it was the bank's motion, so the bank should provide you with an order.

MR. HAHM: Doesn't the prevailing party usually do it, your Honor?

THE COURT: Usually. But we're dealing with pro per, so I usually ask the attorney, as a matter of courtesy, to prepare the order.

MR. HAHM: I will do that.

(Whereupon, the proceeding adjourned at 10:22 a.m.)

STATE OF CALIFORNIA)
)
) ss.
)
COUNTY OF MARIN)

I, Jo Dillingham Brewer, do certify that I am a Certified Shorthand Reporter pursuant to the laws of the State of California;

That acting as such reporter I took down in stenotype the testimony given and proceedings had in the within-held action full, truly, and correct.

That I thereafter caused the foregoing transcript of proceedings of said cause to be transcribed into typewriting, and that the foregoing pages constitute a true and correct transcript of said stenotype so taken.

DATED: San Rafael, California, this 7th day of December, 2012.

JO DILLINGHAM BREWER, CSR NO. 9707

Exhibit M

Order of Marin County Probate Court Appointing Samuel H. Sloan as Administrator of the Estate of K. Michael Goodall with Will Annexed

DE-140

ATTORNEY OR PARTY WITHOUT ATTORNEY (Name, state bar number, and address):	TELEPHONE AND FAX NOS.:	FOR COURT USE ONLY
Samuel H. Sloan 461 Peachstone Terrace San Rafael CA 94903 samhsloan@gmail.com ATTORNEY FOR (Name):	415-894-7201	FILED MAR 2 1 2011 KIM TURNER, Court Executive Officer MARIN COUNTY SUPERIOR COURT By: S. Bond, Deputy
SUPERIOR COURT OF CALIFORNIA, COUNTY OF Marin STREET ADDRESS: 3501 Civic Center Drive MAILING ADDRESS: CITY AND ZIP CODE: San Rafael CA 94903 BRANCH NAME:		
ESTATE OF (Name): K. Michael Goodall DECEDENT		
ORDER FOR PROBATE **ORDER APPOINTING** ☐ **Executor** ☑ **Administrator with Will Annexed** ☐ **Administrator** ☐ **Special Administrator** ☐ **Order Authorizing Independent Administration of Estate** ☐ **with full authority** ☐ **with limited authority**		CASE NUMBER: PR 1100596

WARNING: THIS APPOINTMENT IS NOT EFFECTIVE UNTIL LETTERS HAVE ISSUED.

1. Date of hearing: MAR 2 1 2011 Time: 8:30 am Dept./Room: H Judge: VERNA ADAMS

THE COURT FINDS

2. a. All notices required by law have been given.
   b. Decedent died on (date): October 5, 2010
      (1) ☑ a resident of the California county named above.
      (2) ☐ a nonresident of California and left an estate in the county named above.
   c. Decedent died
      (1) ☐ intestate
      (2) ☑ testate
      and decedent's will dated: January 15, 2004 and each codicil dated:
      was admitted to probate by Minute Order on (date): MAR 2 1 2011

THE COURT ORDERS

3. (Name): Samuel H. Sloan
   is appointed **personal representative:**
   a. ☐ executor of the decedent's will
   b. ☑ administrator with will annexed
   c. ☐ administrator
   d. ☐ special administrator
      (1) ☐ with general powers
      (2) ☐ with special powers as specified in Attachment 3d(2)
      (3) ☐ without notice of hearing
      (4) ☐ letters will expire on (date):

   and letters shall issue on qualification.
4. a. ☑ **Full authority** is granted to administer the estate under the Independent Administration of Estates Act.
   b. ☐ **Limited authority** is granted to administer the estate under the Independent Administration of Estates Act (there is no authority, without court supervision, to (1) sell or exchange real property or (2) grant an option to purchase real property or (3) borrow money with the loan secured by an encumbrance upon real property).
5. a. ☑ Bond is not required.
   b. ☐ Bond is fixed at: $ to be furnished by an authorized surety company or as otherwise provided by law.
   c. ☐ Deposits of: $ are ordered to be placed in a blocked account at (specify institution and location):
      and receipts shall be filed. No withdrawals shall be made without a court order. ☐ Additional orders in Attachment 5c.
   d. ☐ The personal representative is not authorized to take possession of money or any other property without a specific court order.
6. ☐ (Name): is appointed probate referee.

Date: MAR 2 1 2011

VERNA ADAMS
JUDGE OF THE SUPERIOR COURT

7. Number of pages attached: ____ ☐ SIGNATURE FOLLOWS LAST ATTACHMENT

DE-150

ATTORNEY OR PARTY WITHOUT ATTORNEY (Name, state bar number, and address):	TELEPHONE AND FAX NOS.:	FOR COURT USE ONLY
Samuel H. Sloan 461 Peachstone Terrace San Rafael CA 94903 samhsloan@gmail.com	415-894-7201	FILED MAR 2 1 2011 KIM TURNER, Court Executive Officer MARIN COUNTY SUPERIOR COURT By: S. Bond, Deputy
ATTORNEY FOR (Name):		
SUPERIOR COURT OF CALIFORNIA, COUNTY OF Marin STREET ADDRESS: 3501 Civic Center Drive MAILING ADDRESS: CITY AND ZIP CODE: San Rafael CA 94903 BRANCH NAME:		
ESTATE OF (Name): K. Michael Goodall, DECEDENT		
LETTERS ☐ TESTAMENTARY ☐ OF ADMINISTRATION ☑ OF ADMINISTRATION WITH WILL ANNEXED ☐ SPECIAL ADMINISTRATION		CASE NUMBER: PR 1100596

LETTERS

1. ☑ The last will of the decedent named above having been proved, the court appoints *(name)*:
   Samuel H. Sloan
   a. ☐ executor.
   b. ☑ administrator with will annexed.
2. ☐ The court appoints *(name)*:
   a. ☐ administrator of the decedent's estate.
   b. ☐ special administrator of decedent's estate
      (1) ☐ with the special powers specified in the *Order for Probate*.
      (2) ☐ with the powers of a general administrator.
      (3) ☐ letters will expire on *(date)*:
3. ☑ The personal representative is authorized to administer the estate under the Independent Administration of Estates Act ☑ **with full authority**
   ☐ **with limited authority** (no authority, without court supervision, to (1) sell or exchange real property or (2) grant an option to purchase real property or (3) borrow money with the loan secured by an encumbrance upon real property).
4. ☐ The personal representative is not authorized to take possession of money or any other property without a specific court order.

WITNESS, clerk of the court, with seal of the court affixed.

(SEAL) SEAL

Date: MAR 2 1 2011

Clerk, by KIM TURNER

S. BOND
(DEPUTY)

AFFIRMATION

1. ☐ PUBLIC ADMINISTRATOR: No affirmation required (Prob. Code, § 7621(c)).
2. ☑ INDIVIDUAL: **I solemnly affirm** that I will perform the duties of personal representative according to law.
3. ☐ INSTITUTIONAL FIDUCIARY *(name)*:

   I solemnly affirm that the institution will perform the duties of personal representative according to law.
   I make this affirmation for myself as an individual and on behalf of the institution as an officer.
   (Name and title):

4. Executed on *(date)*: MARCH 3, 2011
   at *(place)*: SAN RAFAEL, California.

▶ Samuel H. Sloan
(SIGNATURE)

CERTIFICATION

I certify that this document is a correct copy of the original on file in my office and the letters issued the personal representative appointed above have not been revoked, annulled, or set aside, and are still in full force and effect.

(SEAL)

Date:

Clerk, by

(DEPUTY)

Exhibit N

Second Amendment of the Goodall Trust intending to make K. Michael Goodall Trustee of the Trust of September 12, 1990 dated January 19, 1999

SECOND AMENDMENT TO GOODALL TRUST

Preamble. RACHEL A. GOODALL is the settlor of GOODALL TRUST created under that certain declaration dated September 12, 1990, as amended August 24, 1994. RACHEL A. GOODALL is the trustee duly appointed and acting under and by terms of that declaration. In Section 3.3 of Article Three of that declaration, the settlor reserved the right to amend the trust "(d)uring the trustors' joint lifetimes ...." The surviving settlor now wishes to exercise her right of amendment and, to that end, does hereby amend that declaration in the terms stated below. The trustees hereby consent to the terms of this amendment.

1. Amendment of Section 7.1. of Article Seven. Section 7.1. of Article Seven of that declaration is amended to read as follows:

> 7.1. Remaining Settlor-Trustee Serves Alone. On the death of the deceased settlor, or if, for any reason, before that time either settlor ceases to act as trustee, no successor cotrustee shall be appointed to act with regards to the Bypass Trust. Rather, the remaining settlor trustee named in Article One shall have full power to act as trustee of the Bypass Trust and to complete the trust administration.
>
> After the death of the deceased settlor, at the discretion of the surviving settlor, KENNETH MICHAEL GOODALL, may be appointed to act as cotrustee with regards to the Survivors Trust. This appointment shall be confirmed by KENNETH MICHAEL GOODALL signing a

document, such as an Amendment to Declaration of Trust, in which he agrees to be bound by the terms of the trust.

2. Ratification of Other Terms of Trust. In every other respect, the settlor confirms and ratifies the terms of the trust as stated in that certain declaration dated September 12, 1990, as amended August 24, 1994.

3. Execution. We certify that we have read the foregoing declaration of trust, as amended, and that it correctly states the terms and conditions under which the trust estate is to be held, administered, and distributed. As trustees of the trusts created by this declaration of trust, we approve this declaration of trust, as amended, in all particulars, and agree to be bound by its terms and conditions. RACHEL A. GOODALL, as settlor of the trusts created by this declaration of trust, approves this declaration of trust in all particulars, and agrees to be bound by its terms and conditions.

Executed on JAN 19 1999 at Novato, California.

SETTLOR-TRUSTEE

Rachel A. Goodall

RACHEL A. GOODALL

TRUSTEE

K. Michael Goodall

KENNETH MICHAEL GOODALL

ACKNOWLEDGMENT

STATE OF CALIFORNIA)
) ss
COUNTY OF MARIN)

On JAN 19 1999, before me, a notary public in and for the State of California, personally appeared KENNETH MICHAEL GOODALL and RACHEL A. GOODALL, personally known to me (or proved to me on the basis of satisfactory evidence) to be the persons whose names are subscribed to the within instrument, and acknowledged to me that they executed the same in their individual capacities, and that by their signatures on the instrument, the persons executed the instrument.

WITNESS my hand and official seal.

Signature ______________________ (SEAL)

JAMES R. HASTINGS
Commission # 1154713
Notary Public - California
Marin County

Exhibit O

The Goodall Trust dated September 12, 1990

THE GOODALL TRUST

ARTICLE ONE

INTRODUCTION

1.1. Declaration. This trust declaration is made by KENNETH F. GOODALL and RACHEL A. GOODALL, both of Marin County, California, who are herein referred to as "the trustors" or "the trustee," depending on the context. The term "trustee," as used herein, also refers to each successor trustee who is serving as a trustee of a trust created under this instrument. This trust shall be known as the GOODALL TRUST.

ARTICLE TWO

THE TRUST ESTATE

2.1. Definition of Trust Estate. The property described in any schedule that is part of this instrument, the property hereafter transferred to any trust created under this instrument, and the income and proceeds attributable to all such property shall constitute the "trust estate," which shall be held in trust, administered, and distributed according to the terms of this instrument.

2.2. Initial Trust Corpus. The trust estate shall be comprised initially of the property described in the "Schedule of Community Property Assets," which is attached hereto and made a

EXHIBIT A

A

part of this trust instrument. The property described in that schedule is the trustors' community property.

2.3. Character of Property Retained. All property that now is or hereafter becomes part of the trust estate shall retain its character as community property, quasi-community property, or separate property, as the case may be, despite the transfer in trust.

2.4. Trustee's Powers in Community Property. Notwithstanding any other provision of this instrument, during the joint lifetimes of the trustors, the trustee shall not have powers beyond those granted either spouse under California Civil Code sections 5125 and 5127.

ARTICLE THREE

RIGHTS RESERVED TO TRUSTORS

3.1. Additions to the Trust Estate. A trustor or any other person may make inter vivos or testamentary transfers of property to the trustee. That additional property transferred by any other person shall become part of the trust estate upon written acceptance of it by the trustee.

3.2. Power of Revocation While Both Trustors Are Living. During the trustors' joint lifetimes, the trust may be revoked, in whole or in part, as provided in this paragraph.

(a) Community Property. Either trustor acting alone, or both of the trustors acting jointly, shall have the power to revoke the portion of the trust estate that is the trustors' community property. Upon revocation, the trustee shall pay to either trustor or to both trustors, as the trustors' community property, the community property portion of the trust estate that has been revoked.

(b) Separate Property and Quasi-Community Property. A trustor whose separate property or quasi-community property comprises any portion of the trust estate shall have the power to revoke that portion of the trust estate. Upon revocation, the trustee shall pay to the revoking trustor, as his or her separate or quasi-community property, the separate property or quasi-community property portion of the trust estate that has been revoked.

3.3. Power of Amendment While Both Trustors Are Living. During the trustors' joint lifetimes, the trust may be amended, in whole or in part, by both trustors acting jointly.

3.4. Power of Revocation and Power of Amendment After Death of First Trustor to Die. After the death of the first trustor to die, the surviving trustor shall have the power to revoke or amend, in whole or in part, the Survivor's Trust. All other trusts created under this instrument shall become irrevocable and shall not be subject to amendment after the death of the first trustor to die.

3.5. Method of Revocation or Amendment. The revocation or amendment of a trust created under this instrument shall be effective only if made in a writing that is signed by the person or persons having the power of revocation or amendment and delivered to the trustee. An exercise of the power of amendment substantially affecting the duties, rights, and liabilities of the trustee shall be effective only if agreed to by the trustee in writing.

3.6. Incompetent Trustor May Not Act. A power reserved to a trustor under this article may not be exercised by that trustor or by any other person or fiduciary, including the conservator of that trustor's estate or that trustor's attorney in fact designated in a durable power of attorney under the Uniform Durable Power of Attorney Act, if that trustor is incompetent (as defined in Article Nine) at the pertinent time. A power under this article that is exercisable only by the joint action of the trustors may not be exercised if either trustor is incompetent at the pertinent time. However, the incompetence of one trustor shall not prevent a competent trustor from exercising a power that is exercisable by the competent trustor acting alone.

ARTICLE FOUR

DISTRIBUTIONS DURING TRUSTORS' JOINT LIVES

4.1. Payment of Income During Trustors' Joint Lives. So long as both trustors are living, the trustee shall pay the net income of the trust as specified in this paragraph.

(a) Community Property. The trustee shall pay to either trustor or both trustors or apply for the trustors' benefit the entire net income from the trust community property, in monthly or other convenient installments (but not less often than annually) as either or both of the trustors and the trustee may agree upon from time to time.

(b) Separate Property and Quasi-Community Property. The trustee shall pay to or apply for the benefit of a trustor whose separate property or quasi-community property comprises part of the trust estate the entire net income from that separate property or quasi-community property, in monthly or other convenient installments (but not less often than annually) as that trustor and the trustee may agree upon from time to time.

4.2. Discretionary Payment of Principal by Trustee During Trustors' Joint Lives. So long as both trustors are living, the trustee shall pay trust principal, at any time or times, as specified in this paragraph.

(a) <u>Community Property</u>. The trustee shall pay to either trustor or both trustors or apply for the trustors' benefit so much of the principal of the trust community property as the trustee deems proper for the comfort, welfare, and happiness of the trustor or trustors.

(b) <u>Separate Property and Quasi-Community Property</u>. The trustee shall pay to or apply for the benefit of a trustor whose separate property or quasi-community property comprises part of the trust estate so much of the principal of that separate property or quasi-community property as the trustee deems proper for that trustor's comfort, welfare, and happiness.

(c) <u>Consideration of Other Resources When Distributing Principal</u>. In exercising discretion under subparagraphs (a) and (b) of this paragraph, the trustee shall give the consideration that the trustee deems proper to all other income and resources then readily available for use by the trustor or trustors, as the case may be, for the stated purposes and that are then known to the trustee. All decisions of the trustee regarding payments under subparagraph (a) or (b), if any, are within the trustee's discretion and shall be final and incontestable by anyone.

4.3. <u>Trustors' Right to Withdraw Principal</u>. So long as both trustors are living, the trustors shall have the right to withdraw trust principal, at any time or times, as specified in this paragraph.

(a) <u>Community Property</u>. Either trustor acting alone, if he or she is not incompetent (as defined in Article Nine) at the pertinent time, or both of the trustors acting jointly, if at least one of them is not incompetent at the pertinent time, shall have the right to withdraw any amount of trust principal that is the trustors' community property, by delivering a signed writing to the trustee.

(b) <u>Separate Property and Quasi-Community Property</u>. A trustor whose separate property or quasi-community property comprises part of the trust estate, if not incompetent (as defined in Article Nine) at the pertinent time, shall have the right to withdraw any amount of the principal of that separate property or quasi-community property, by delivering a signed writing to the trustee.

4.4. Trustors' Obligation for Community Property Received or Withdrawn. Net income of the trust community property paid to either trustor or both trustors pursuant to the provisions of this article and principal of the trust community property distributed to or withdrawn by either trustor or both trustors pursuant to the provisions of this article shall remain the trustors' community property. A trustor who receives such net income or principal shall have the same obligations respecting that property as he or she would have with regard to all community property generally.

ARTICLE FIVE

DIVISION INTO SHARES AND INITIAL DISTRIBUTIONS AFTER DECEASED SPOUSE'S DEATH

5.1. Definitions. In this article and subsequent articles of this instrument, the first trustor to die is referred to as "the deceased spouse" and the other trustor is referred to as "the surviving spouse."

5.2. Trustee's Power to Defer Division or Distribution. Whenever the trustee is directed to divide any part of the trust estate or distribute trust assets upon the death of either trustor, the trustee may, in the trustee's discretion, defer actual division or distribution for a period not exceeding six (6) months after that trustor's death. The ability of the trustee to delay division or distribution shall not affect the vesting of interests in the respective shares, which shall be as of the date of death.

5.3. Division Into Three Shares After Death of Deceased Spouse. Upon the death of the deceased spouse, the trustee shall divide the trust estate, including any additions made to the trust by reason of the deceased spouse's death, such as from the deceased spouse's estate or policies of life insurance on his or her life, into three separate shares, designated "the survivor's share," "the marital deduction share," and "the credit shelter share," to be held, administered, or distributed as set forth below.

5.4. Payment of Death Taxes, Debts, and Expenses. After the death of the deceased spouse, upon receipt by the trustee of a written statement from the personal representative of the deceased spouse's estate requesting that the trustee pay death taxes, debts, and expenses (as defined in Article Nine), with respect to assets of any trust under this instrument or other taxable property or transfers, the trustee shall pay out of the trust estate, either directly or to the personal representative, any amounts requested by the personal representative for those purposes. The trustee may rely upon the personal representative's statement and shall not be liable for any act or omission by the personal representative in protesting or failing to protest the legality, propriety, or amount of the death taxes, debts, or expenses. The trustee shall pay as much of the federal estate tax as possible with any "flower bonds" (United States Treasury obligations acceptable at par value in payment of federal estate tax) that are part of the trust estate, but only to the extent of the deceased spouse's interest in those bonds. Payment of death taxes and payment of expenses shall be charged to the credit shelter share, except for any death taxes that are attributable to a disclaimer of property under this instrument by the surviving spouse, which shall be paid from the Disclaimer Trust. Payment of any debts allocable against the separate property of the deceased spouse shall be charged against the credit shelter share. Debts allocable against community property shall be allocated to the survivor's share and the credit shelter share in accordance with California law in effect at the date of the deceased spouse's death, so long as charges against the survivor's share do not exceed the value of community property allocable to that share. The trustee shall not pay death taxes, debts, and expenses or other obligations of the deceased spouse or the deceased spouse's estate from proceeds of insurance policies on the deceased spouse's life if making those payments would be the sole cause of the proceeds being includable in the deceased spouse's gross estate for federal estate tax purposes.

5.5. Survivor's Share Allocated to Survivor's Trust. The survivor's share, as determined in this paragraph, shall be held, administered, and distributed by the trustee according to the terms set forth in Article Six applicable to the Survivor's Trust, for the benefit of the surviving spouse. The survivor's share shall consist of the portion of the trust estate that is comprised of the surviving spouse's one-half (1/2) interest in the trustors' community property, the surviving spouse's one-half (1/2) interest in the deceased spouse's quasi-community property, all of the surviving spouse's separate property, and all of the surviving spouse's quasi-community property.

5.6. <u>Credit Shelter Share Allocated to Credit Shelter Trust</u>. The credit shelter share, as determined in this paragraph, shall be held, administered, and distributed by the trustee according to the terms set forth in Article Six applicable to the Credit Shelter Trust. The credit shelter share shall consist of a pecuniary gift from the trust estate other than the survivor's share (as defined in the preceding paragraph) that is the largest amount, if any, of property that can pass free of federal estate tax by reason of (1) the unified credit available to the deceased spouse's estate; and (2) the credit for state death taxes, to the extent that the use of that credit does not result in or increase any death tax payable to any state. Any qualified disclaimer made by the surviving spouse shall be disregarded in determining this amount. The trustors recognize that the amount of this pecuniary gift may be affected by a number of considerations, including:

(a) The net value of all property disposed of by this instrument or otherwise that is included in the deceased spouse's gross estate for federal estate tax purposes and that does not qualify for the federal estate tax marital or charitable deduction;

(b) The value of all property disposed of by the deceased spouse that constitutes "adjusted taxable gifts";

(c) All charges to principal that are deductible under Internal Revenue Code section 2053 but that are not deducted in computing the federal estate tax liability for the deceased spouse's gross estate; and

(d) Actions of the deceased spouse's executor in exercising certain tax elections.

The trustors recognize that because of the above factors no property may pass pursuant to this provision.

5.7. Marital Deduction Share Distributed Outright. The marital deduction share shall consist of the balance of the trust estate, and shall be distributed outright to the surviving spouse.

5.8. Allocation of Assets. In allocating assets between the marital deduction share and the credit shelter share, the trustee shall allocate the assets in the trust estate that qualify for the marital deduction between the marital deduction share and the credit shelter share in cash or in kind, or partly in each, on a prorata or a nonprorata basis, and in undivided interests or not, but subject to the following:

(a) Qualification for Marital Deduction. Only assets that qualify for the marital deduction shall be allocated to the marital deduction share.

(b) Allocations in Kind. Assets allocated in kind shall be valued for purposes of allocation on the date or dates of distribution.

(c) Foreign Death Tax Credit. Assets that qualify for the foreign death tax credit shall be allocated to the marital deduction share only if other trust property is insufficient to fund the marital deduction share.

5.9. Intention That Disposition of Marital Deduction Share Qualify for Marital Deduction. The trustors intend that the disposition of the marital deduction share qualify for the federal estate tax marital deduction and that the trustee take no action or exercise any power that may impair that deduction. The trustors incorporate in this instrument the provisions of California Probate Code section 21522.

5.10. Disclaimer of Property by Surviving Spouse. Any property or portion thereof that is disclaimed by the surviving spouse shall be held, administered, or distributed by the trustee according to the terms set forth in Article Six applicable to the Disclaimer Trust.

ARTICLE SIX

DISPOSITIVE PROVISIONS OF TRUSTS CREATED AFTER DECEASED SPOUSE'S DEATH

6.1. Survivor's Trust. The property allocated to the Survivor's Trust shall be held, administered, and distributed for the benefit of the surviving spouse according to the following terms and conditions:

(a) Payment of Income. The trustee shall pay to or apply for the benefit of the surviving spouse, so long as the surviving spouse lives, the entire net income of the trust, in monthly or other convenient installments (but not less often than annually) as the surviving spouse and the trustee may agree upon from time to time.

(b) Discretionary Payment of Principal by Trustee. At any time or times during the trust term, the trustee shall pay to or apply for the benefit of the surviving spouse so much of the principal of the trust as the trustee deems proper for the surviving spouse's comfort, welfare, and happiness. In exercising discretion, the trustee shall give the consideration that the trustee deems proper to all other income and resources then readily available to the surviving spouse for use for these purposes and that are then known to the trustee. All decisions of the trustee regarding payments under this subparagraph, if any, are within the trustee's discretion and shall be final and incontestable by anyone.

(c) Right of Surviving Spouse to Withdraw Principal. The trustee shall pay to the surviving spouse as much of the trust principal as the surviving spouse may from time to time demand in a signed writing delivered to the trustee.

(d) General Power of Appointment. Upon the death of the surviving spouse, all of the trust property (including the trust principal, all net income then held by the trustee, and all income then accrued but not collected by the trustee) shall be paid over and delivered to any entity or entities, person or persons, and upon any trust, terms and conditions, or to or in favor of the estate of the surviving spouse, as the surviving spouse may direct by will, provided only that no exercise of this power of appointment shall be effective unless it refers to this instrument and expressly indicates an intention to exercise this power of appointment. The trustee may rely upon any instrument admitted to probate as the last will of the surviving spouse in carrying out the terms of the power of appointment and shall not be liable for any good-faith act in reliance upon that will, even if for any reason it is later determined to be invalid with respect to its purported exercise of this power of appointment. If the trustee receives no notice of the existence of a will of the surviving spouse within six (6) months after the death of the surviving spouse, the trustee may distribute the trust assets and income as though this power of appointment had not been exercised and shall in that event be conclusively presumed to have acted in good faith, even if a valid will is thereafter discovered.

(e) Payment of Death Taxes, Debts, and Expenses. On the death of the surviving spouse and subject to any power of appointment exercised by him or her, the trustee may, in the trustee's discretion, pay out of the income or principal or partly from the income and partly from the principal of the Survivor's Trust, the death taxes, debts, and expenses (as defined in Article Nine) arising on the death of the surviving spouse.

(f) Default Provision. In default of the power of appointment, or to the extent that an attempt to exercise the power was ineffectual, the entire remaining principal, all net income then held by the trustee, and all income then accrued but not collected by the trustee, after any payment of taxes, debts, and expenses pursuant to the applicable provisions of this instrument, shall be disposed of in the manner specified in the paragraph below entitled "Disposition of Credit Shelter Trust Upon Death of Surviving Spouse," although the property disposed of pursuant to this subparagraph shall not be considered to be part of the Credit Shelter Trust.

6.2. Disposition of Credit Shelter Trust Until Death of Surviving Spouse. The property allocated to the Credit Shelter Trust shall be held, administered, and distributed until the death of the surviving spouse according to the following terms and conditions:

(a) Discretionary Payment of Income and Principal by Trustee. At any time or times, the trustee shall pay to or apply for the benefit of the surviving spouse so much of the net income and principal of the trust as the trustee deems proper for the health, education, support, and maintenance of the surviving spouse. In exercising discretion, the trustee shall give the consideration that the trustee deems proper to all other income and resources then readily available to the surviving spouse for use for these purposes and that are then known to the trustee. All decisions of the trustee regarding payments under this subparagraph, if any, are within the trustee's discretion and shall be final and incontestable by anyone. Any net income not expended under the foregoing provisions of this subparagraph shall be accumulated and added to the principal of the trust.

(b) Right of Surviving Spouse to Withdraw Principal. The surviving spouse shall have the power to withdraw from the principal of the trust each calendar year those amounts as shall not exceed the greater of five thousand dollars ($5,000) or five (5) percent of the assets, valued as of the end of the calendar year. The surviving spouse shall exercise this power by a written instrument signed by him or her and delivered to the trustee. This power is noncumulative and to the extent it is not exercised by the end of the calendar year, it shall lapse. This power shall exist each year until the death of the surviving spouse.

6.3. Disposition of Credit Shelter Trust Upon Death of Surviving Spouse. Upon the death of the surviving spouse, the property in the Credit Shelter Trust shall be disposed of as follows:

(a) To KENNETH MICHAEL GOODALL, by right of representation, those issue to take that share in the manner provided in California Probate Code section 240.

(b) If the property is not completely disposed of by the preceding provisions, twenty thousand dollars ($20,000.00) to each of the living brothers and sisters of the trustors and the remainder to GUIDE DOGS FOR THE BLIND OF MARIN, INC., of San Rafael, California.

(c) If the property is not completely disposed of by the preceding provisions, the trustee shall pay over and deliver the undisposed portion outright as follows: one-half (1/2) to the heirs of the deceased spouse and one-half (1/2) to the heirs of the surviving spouse.

6.4. Disclaimer Trust. The property allocated to the Disclaimer Trust shall be held, administered, and distributed according to the following terms and conditions:

(a) Payment of Income. The trustee shall pay to or apply for the benefit of the surviving spouse the entire net income of the trust, in monthly or other convenient installments (but not less often than annually) as the surviving spouse and the trustee may agree upon from time to time.

(b) Payment of Principal. At any time or times, the trustee shall pay to or apply for the benefit of the surviving spouse so much of the principal of the trust as the trustee deems proper for the health, education, support, and maintenance of the surviving spouse. In exercising discretion, the trustee shall give the consideration that the trustee deems proper to all other income and resources then readily available to the surviving spouse for use for these purposes and that are then known to the trustee.

(c) Distribution of Remainder. Upon the death of the surviving spouse, the remaining trust property (including all income then accrued but uncollected and all net income then remaining in the hands of the trustee) shall be disposed of in the manner specified in the preceding paragraph, entitled "Disposition of Credit Shelter Trust Upon Death of Surviving Spouse," although the property disposed of pursuant to this subparagraph shall not be considered to be part of the Credit Shelter Trust.

ARTICLE SEVEN

OFFICE OF TRUSTEE

7.1. Remaining Trustor-Trustee Serves Alone. Upon the death of the deceased spouse, or if before that time either trustor resigns as trustee, is removed pursuant to judicial procedure, becomes incompetent (as defined in Article Nine), or for any reason fails or ceases to act as trustee, the remaining trustor-trustee shall serve as sole trustee.

7.2. Successor Trustees. Upon the death of the remaining trustor-trustee, or if the remaining trustor-trustee resigns as trustee, is removed pursuant to judicial procedure, becomes incompetent, or for any reason fails or ceases to act as trustee,

KENNETH MICHAEL GOODALL shall become the trustee. If KENNETH MICHAEL GOODALL is not qualified for appointment as trustee, or if he later dies, resigns, is removed pursuant to judicial procedure, or for any reason fails or ceases to act as trustee, SECURITY PACIFIC BANK shall serve as the corporate sole trustee.

7.3. Waiver of Bond of Individual Trustees. No bond shall be required of any individual who serves as a trustee under this instrument.

7.4. Trustee's Right and Method of Resignation. Any trustee may resign at any time, without giving a reason for the resignation, by executing a signed written instrument and delivering it to any other trustee then acting, to the successor trustee designated in the manner provided in this article, to the trustors, if living, and if either trustor is deceased, to the trust beneficiaries. A resignation shall be effective upon written acceptance of the trust by the successor trustee.

7.5. Trustee's Liability. The trustee shall not be liable to any person with an interest in the trust for acts or omissions of the trustee, except those resulting from willful misconduct or gross negligence. This standard shall also apply regarding the trustee's liability for acts or omissions of any co-trustee, predecessor trustee, or agent employed by the trustee.

7.6. Compensation of Corporate Trustee. A corporate trustee shall be entitled to reasonable compensation for services rendered in accordance with its fee schedule in effect from time to time for inter vivos trusts.

the trustee deems advisable, and acquire every kind of investment, real, personal, or mixed, including but not limited to improved and unimproved real property, corporate and government (whether local, state, or federal) obligations of every kind, stocks (both preferred and common), and shares of mutual funds of any character; and (2) retain as an investment for the trust in the same form received by the trustee any property given to the trustee from any source. The trustee is under no duty to diversify the investments of the trust. This paragraph shall be construed as expanding the standards set forth in California Probate Code section 16040.

8.3. Power of Trustee with Regard to Accounts. Initially there will be two persons acting as co-trustees for this Trust. In order to make payments from the Trust without undue complications, the trustees will need to open bank, investment, securities brokerage, margin, and similar accounts in which either trustee may be the signatory. This provision specifically gives to the co-trustees the power to open as many accounts as needed (checking, savings, certificates of deposit, money market accounts, investment, etc.) and open such accounts so that deposits and withdrawals may be made with the signature of only one trustee. This includes the power to open an account where either trustee or only one may sign on the account. The initial trustees are specifically vested with the power and authority to open, operate and maintain these accounts and to use the other powers provided in this trust, such as the power to buy and sell on margin, hypothecate, borrow upon, purchase and/or sell as the sole trustee

7.7. Compensation of Individual Trustees. Each individual who is a trustee under this instrument shall be entitled to reasonable compensation for fiduciary services rendered. The trustee may pay these fees from the funds of the pertinent trust as an expense of trust administration, without court order.

ARTICLE EIGHT

POWERS OF TRUSTEE

8.1. General Powers of Trustee. In order to carry out the purposes of this trust, the trustee shall have all of the powers enumerated herein and, except as limited by any provision of this instrument, all powers now or hereafter granted to a trustee by law. Except as limited by a more specific provision of this instrument, the trustee shall have the power to:

(a) Sell, exchange, transfer, convey, lease without limitation as to term, borrow upon, and hypothecate all or any part of the trust property;

(b) Retain, maintain, repair, divide, partition, improve, and otherwise manage any trust property;

(c) Insure trust property against damage or loss, and against liability with respect to third persons, at the expense of the trust, with the carriers and coverages that the trustee deems advisable;

(d) Enforce the rights of the trust with respect to any mortgage, deed of trust, pledge, or similar security device held in trust; enforce, at a foreclosure sale (whether judicial or nonjudicial) or other sale, the rights of the trust in secured property; make bids upon and purchase, at trust expense, any property that is subject to security device; and accept a deed in lieu of foreclosure as full or complete satisfaction of the secured debt;

(e) Commence or defend, at the expense of the trust, legal actions relating to the trust or any trust property as the trustee deems advisable;

(f) Compromise, submit to arbitration, settle, or release (with or without consideration) or otherwise adjust any claims in favor of or against the trust;

(g) Hold trust property in the name of a nominee or nominees, with or without disclosing the trust character of such property (including securities in such condition that ownership may pass upon delivery), or in the name of the trustee as trustee;

(h) Exercise any and all rights and powers of an owner of stocks or securities; vote and give proxies; pay assessments or other charges; exercise or not exercise, as the trustee deems advisable, subscriptions, conversion rights, or other rights or options that may devolve upon holders of stocks or securities; and enter into shareholder agreements;

(i) Participate in any plans or proceedings for foreclosure or consolidations, merger, liquidation, or other reorganization of any corporation or organization having securities that are held as trust property and, in connection therewith, deposit securities with and transfer title or securities upon the terms that the trustee deems advisable to any protective or other committee established in connection with any such plan or proceeding;

(j) Subdivide and resubdivide trust real property and sign applications, maps, and other documents incidental thereto; to dedicate trust real property for public purposes, with or without consideration; grant and impose upon trust real property, conditions, covenants, easements, restrictions, rights of way, and other servitudes; borrow against trust real property; and do such other acts as may appear to the trustee advisable in connection with the exercise of any of the powers described in this subparagraph.

(k) Receive additions to the trust from any source at any time;

(l) Borrow money for any trust purpose on such terms and conditions as the trustee deems advisable and obligate the trust to repay the borrowing;

(m) Employ attorneys, investment counsel, accountants, bookkeepers, or other persons to render services regarding all matters pertaining to the trusts, and pay from trust property the reasonable compensation of such persons for their services.

8.2. <u>Trustee's Power to Invest and Retain Trust Property</u>. The trustee shall have the power to (1) invest trust property as deems appropriate.

8.4. Trustee's Power Regarding Unproductive Property. The trustee may retain or acquire unproductive or underproductive property. California Probate Code section 16311 shall not apply to any trust created under this instrument.

8.5. Retention of Residence. After the deceased spouse's death, the trustee may retain in any trust or trusts provided for under this instrument, for the personal use of the surviving spouse, any property occupied by the trustors as a principal place of residence at the time of the deceased spouse's death, for as long as the surviving spouse desires to occupy the residence. The trustee shall pay from the trust estate all expenses associated with the maintenance and upkeep of such property. On the written request of the surviving spouse, the trustee may sell the residence and replace it with other property of comparable or lower value suitable as a residence for the surviving spouse. If the surviving spouse becomes subject to a conservatorship of the estate or person, the conservator shall be empowered to act for the surviving spouse.

8.6. Combining Multi-Trust Property. Each trust created under this instrument shall constitute a separate trust and be administered accordingly; however, the assets of all of the trusts may be combined for bookkeeping purposes and held for the trust beneficiaries without physical division into separate trusts until time of distribution.

8.7. Spendthrift Clause. To the maximum extent permitted by

law, the interests of each trust beneficiary under this instrument are not transferable by voluntary or involuntary assignment or by operation of law and shall be free from the claims of creditors and from attachment, execution, bankruptcy, and other legal process. If any such transfer is made or attempted by or against a trust beneficiary, all further trust payments of income or principal or both to that beneficiary (and any right of that beneficiary to such payments) shall be suspended for a period of time or indefinitely (but in no case for longer than the term of the trust) as the trustee determines. In lieu of payments to the beneficiary, the trustee may apply so much of the trust income or principal or both to which the beneficiary would otherwise be entitled as the trustee deems necessary for the beneficiary's education and support. All trust income (to which the beneficiary would otherwise be entitled) not so applied shall in the discretion of the trustee be accumulated and added to trust principal at such time or times as the trustee deems proper.

8.8. Division or Distribution in Cash or Kind. Except to the extent that any provisions in this instrument that specify the allocation of assets involving the marital deduction conflict with this paragraph, the trustee, in order to satisfy a pecuniary gift or to distribute or divide trust assets into shares or partial shares, may distribute or divide such assets in kind, or divide undivided interests in such assets, or sell all or any part of such assets and distribute or divide the property in cash, in kind, or partly in cash and partly in kind. Property distributed to satisfy a pecuniary gift under this instrument shall be valued at its fair market value at the time of distribution.

8.9. Payments on Behalf of Minors or Persons Under Disability. If at any time any beneficiary is a minor or it appears to the trustee that any beneficiary is disabled, incompetent, or for any other reason not able to receive payments or make intelligent or responsible use of the payments, then the trustee, in lieu of making direct payments to the beneficiary, may make payments to the beneficiary's conservator or guardian; to the beneficiary's custodian under the Uniform Gifts to Minors Act or Uniform Transfers to Minors Act of any state; to one or more suitable persons as the trustee deems proper, such as a relative of the beneficiary or a person residing with the beneficiary, to be used for the beneficiary's benefit; to any other person, firm, or agency for services rendered or to be rendered for the beneficiary's assistance or benefit; or to accounts in the beneficiary's name with financial institutions. The receipt of payments by any of the foregoing shall constitute a sufficient acquittance of the trustee for all purposes.

8.10. Trustee's Duty to Account. The trustee shall not be required to render periodic accounts to any person, but shall render accounts at the termination of a trust and upon a change of trustee, to the persons and in the manner required by law.

8.11. Written Notice to Trustee. Until the trustee receives written notice of any death or other event upon which the right to payments from any trust may depend, the trustee shall incur no liability for disbursements made in good faith to persons whose interests may have been affected by that event.

8.12. <u>No Early Termination of Trust Without Prior Court Authorization</u>. California Probate Code section 15408(b) shall not apply to any trust under this instrument, and except as otherwise provided in this instrument, the trustee may not terminate a trust before the trust term expires unless prior court authorization is obtained.

ARTICLE NINE

CONCLUDING PROVISIONS

9.1. <u>Perpetuities Savings Clause</u>. Unless sooner terminated, each trust created by this instrument shall terminate twenty-one (21) years after the later of (1) the death of the last to die of the trustors' issue who are living at the death of the surviving spouse, or (2) the death of the surviving spouse. If a trust is terminated because of the preceding sentence, the trustee shall distribute the trust property outright pro rata, to the persons who are then entitled or eligible to receive trust income (or if there are no such persons, outright in a manner that the trustee believes will give effect to the trustors' intent in creating the trust).

9.2. <u>Period of Survivorship</u>. For the purposes of this instrument, a beneficiary shall not be deemed to have survived a trustor if that beneficiary dies within sixty (60) days after the trustor's death.

9.3. <u>Severability Clause</u>. If any provision of this

instrument is invalid, that provision shall be disregarded and shall not affect any of the other provisions.

9.4. <u>Captions</u>. The captions appearing in this instrument are for convenience of reference only and shall have no significance in the construction or interpretation of this instrument.

9.5. <u>Definition of Heirs</u>. Any reference to a trustor's "heirs" in the dispositive provisions of this instrument shall be construed as referring to those persons who are entitled to that trustor's property under the laws of intestate succession in effect at the time of execution of this instrument.

9.6. <u>Definitions of Issue, Child, and Children</u>. The terms "issue," "child," and "children," when used in the dispositive provisions of this instrument, shall be given the meanings accorded those terms in Part 2 of Division 1 of the California Probate Code in effect at the time of execution of this instrument.

9.7. <u>Definition of Incompetent</u>. For all purposes under this instrument, a person shall be deemed "incompetent" if and so long as a conservator of his or her person or estate duly appointed by a court of competent jurisdiction is serving, or upon certification by two physicians (licensed to practice under the laws of the state where the person is domiciled) that the person is unable properly to care for himself or herself, for his or her person, or for his or her property.

9.8. <u>Definition of Death Taxes, Debts, and Expenses</u>. As used in this instrument, the term "death taxes, debts, and expenses" shall include the following:

(a) All estate, inheritance, succession, and similar taxes (including any interest and penalties) that become payable by reason of a trustor's death or by any person on account of that person's interest in that trustor's estate, but excluding any federal or state tax imposed on any "generation-skipping transfer," and excluding any addition to the federal estate tax for any "excess retirement accumulation" under Internal Revenue Code section 4980A.

(b) All costs, expenses of litigation, counsel fees, or other charges that the trustee incurs in connection with the determination of the amount of the taxes, interest, or penalties referred to in subparagraph (a) of this paragraph; and

(c) Legally enforceable debts, funeral expenses, expenses of last illness, and administration and property expenses.

9.9. California Trust Law to Apply. California law shall govern the validity, interpretation, and administration of any trust created under this instrument, regardless of the domicile of any trustee or beneficiary.

ARTICLE TEN

EXECUTION

10.1. Execution. We, and each of us, certify that we have read the foregoing trust declaration and that it correctly states the terms and conditions under which the trust estate is to be held, managed, and disposed of by the trustees. We approve of the trust declaration in all particulars, and as the trustees named in the trust declaration, accept the trusts provided for in the declaration.

10.2. Executed on SEP 12 1990 at San Anselmo, California.

KENNETH F. GOODALL

RACHEL A. GOODALL

ACKNOWLEDGMENT

STATE OF CALIFORNIA)
) ss
COUNTY OF MARIN)

On SEP 12 1990 before me, the undersigned officer, personally appeared KENNETH F. GOODALL and RACHEL A. GOODALL, personally known to me (or proved to me on the basis of satisfactory evidence) to be the persons whose names are subscribed to this instrument, and acknowledged that they executed it.

Notary Public

(SEAL)

...CIAL SEAL
JAMES R. HASTINGS
Notary Public-California
MARIN COUNTY
My Commission Expires
August 20, 1993

SCHEDULE OF COMMUNITY PROPERTY ASSETS

1. The real property commonly known as 461 Peachstone Terrace, San Rafael, California, and specifically known as:

> Lot No. 1068, "Map of Marinwood Unit 7", County of Marin, Initially recorded 19 ct. 1959 in Map Book #10, Page 42, Marin County records.

Exhibit P

Purported Last Will of Kenneth F. Goodall

LAST WILL OF
KENNETH F. GOODALL

I, KENNETH F. GOODALL, a resident of Marin County, California, declare that this is my will. I hereby revoke all my previous wills and codicils.

ARTICLE ONE

INTRODUCTORY PROVISIONS

1.1. Marital Status. I am married to RACHEL A. GOODALL, and all references in this will to "my wife" are to her.

1.2. Identification of Living Child. I have one living child, KENNETH MICHAEL GOODALL.

1.3. No Deceased Children. I have no deceased children.

ARTICLE TWO

RESIDUARY PROVISIONS

2.1. Disposition of Residue. I give the residue of my estate to the trustee of the GOODALL TRUST, created under the declaration of trust executed on September 12, 1990, by KENNETH F. GOODALL and RACHEL A. GOODALL, as Settlors and Trustees. The trustee of that trust shall add the residue of my estate to the trust principal and hold, administer, and distribute the property in accordance with the provisions of that declaration of trust, including any amendments of that declaration of trust that have been made before or after execution of this will.

2.2. Alternate Disposition of Residue. If the GOODALL TRUST has been revoked, terminated, or declared invalid for any reason, I give the portion of the residue of my estate not taken to the executor of this will, as trustee, who shall hold, administer, and distribute the property under a testamentary trust, the terms of which shall be identical to the terms of the GOODALL TRUST that are in effect on the date of execution of this will.

ARTICLE THREE

EXECUTOR

3.1. Nomination of Executors. I nominate my wife as executor of this will. If, for any reason, my wife fails to qualify or ceases to act as executor, I nominate BANK OF AMERICA, NT & SA, San Francisco, California, or any corporation that is a successor thereto by merger, consolidation, transfer of assets, or other manner provided by law, as executor of this will.

3.2. Waiver of Bond. No bond or undertaking shall be required of any executor nominated in this will.

3.3. General Powers of Executor. The executor shall have full authority to administer my estate under the California Independent Administration of Estates Act. The executor shall have all powers now or hereafter conferred on executors by law, except as otherwise specifically provided in this will, including any powers enumerated in this will.

3.4. Power to Invest. The executor shall have the power to

invest estate funds in any kind of real or personal property, as the executor deems advisable.

3.5. Division or Distribution in Cash or in Kind. In order to satisfy a pecuniary gift or to distribute or divide estate assets into shares or partial shares, the executor may distribute or divide those assets in kind, or divide undivided interests in those assets, or sell all or any part of those assets and distribute or divide the property in cash, in kind, or partly in cash and partly in kind. Property distributed to satisfy a pecuniary gift under this will shall be valued at its fair market value at the time of distribution.

3.6. Power to Sell, Lease, and Grant Options to Purchase Property. The executor shall have the power to sell, at either public or private sale and with or without notice, lease, and grant options to purchase any real or personal property belonging to my estate, on such terms and conditions as the executor determines to be in the best interest of my estate.

3.7. Power to Purchase Estate Property. The executor shall have the power to sell any property of my estate to, or exchange any property of my estate with the property of, my wife, even though she is also an executor at the time of the sale or exchange, provided that any such sale or exchange shall be for adequate consideration.

3.8. Payments to Legally Incapacitated Persons. If at any time any beneficiary under this will is a minor or it appears to the executor that any beneficiary is incapacitated, incompetent, or for any other reason not able to receive payments or make intelligent or responsible use of the payments, then the executor, in lieu of making direct payments to the beneficiary, may make payments to the beneficiary's conservator or guardian; to the beneficiary's custodian under the Uniform Gifts to Minors Act or Uniform Transfers to Minors Act of any state; to one or more suitable persons, as the executor deems proper, such as a relative or a person residing with the beneficiary, to be used for the benefit of the beneficiary; to any other person, firm, or agency for services rendered or to be rendered for the beneficiary's assistance or benefit; or to accounts in the beneficiary's name with financial institutions. The receipt of payments by any of the foregoing shall constitute a sufficient acquittance of the executor for all purposes.

ARTICLE FOUR

CONCLUDING PROVISIONS

4.1. Nonprobate Transfers of Community Property. If I predecease my wife, I revoke any consent I have given during my lifetime to any nonprobate transfer on the death of any person, to anyone other than my wife, of all or part of my community property interest in any asset described in California Probate Code Section 5000 (or any successor section), and instead I give to my wife my community property interest in any assets affected by this revocation of consent. Notwithstanding the preceding sentence, this revocation of consent shall be inapplicable to any community property included in any express trust of which I am the settlor or a cosettlor, which shall continue to be governed by the terms of the applicable trust instrument. It is my intention that my wife shall have full power to dispose of all community property assets to which this section of the will applies. If my wife and I die simultaneously or if it cannot be established by clear and convincing evidence whether my wife or I died first, this section shall not apply.

4.2. Definition of Death Taxes. The term "death taxes," as used in this will, shall mean all inheritance, estate, succession, and other similar taxes that are payable by any person on account of that person's interest in my estate or by reason of my death, including penalties and interest, but excluding the following:

(a) Any addition to the federal estate tax for any "excess retirement accumulation" under Internal Revenue Code Section 4980A.

(b) Any additional tax that may be assessed under Internal Revenue Code Section 2032A.

(c) Any federal or state tax imposed on a "generation-skipping transfer," as that term is defined in the federal tax laws, unless the applicable tax statutes provide that the generation-skipping transfer tax on that transfer is payable directly out of the assets of my gross estate.

4.3. Payment of Death Taxes. Pursuant to the declaration of trust executed on September 12, 1990, by KENNETH F. GOODALL and RACHEL A. GOODALL, as Settlors and Trustees, all death taxes, whether or not attributable to property inventoried in my probate estate, shall be paid by the trustee from that trust. However, if that trust does not exist at the time of my death, or if the assets of that trust are insufficient to pay the death taxes in full, I direct the executor to pay any death taxes that cannot be paid by the trustee from the assets of my probate estate by prorating and apportioning those taxes among the beneficiaries of this will, as provided in the California Probate Code.

4.4. Period of Survivorship. For the purposes of this will, a beneficiary shall not be deemed to have survived me if that beneficiary dies within forty (40) days after my death.

4.5. No-Contest Clause. If any person, directly or indirectly, contests the validity of this will in whole or in part, or opposes, objects to, or seeks to invalidate any of its provisions, or seeks to succeed to any part of my estate otherwise than in the manner specified in this will, any gift or other interest given to that person under this will shall be revoked and shall be disposed of as if he or she had predeceased me without issue.

4.6. Captions. The captions appearing in this will are for convenience of reference only, and shall be disregarded in determining the meaning and effect of the provisions of this will.

4.7. Severability Clause. If any provision of this will is invalid, that provision shall be disregarded, and the remainder of this will shall be construed as if the invalid provision had not been included.

4.8. California Law to Apply. All questions concerning the

validity and interpretation of this will, including any trusts created by this will, shall be governed by the laws of the State of California in effect at the time this will is executed.

Executed on 8/24/94, at San Rafael, California.

KENNETH F. GOODALL

On the date written above, we, the undersigned, each being present at the same time, witnessed the signing of this instrument by KENNETH F. GOODALL. At that time, KENNETH F. GOODALL appeared to us to be of sound mind and memory and, to the best of our knowledge, was not acting under fraud, duress, menace, or undue influence. Understanding this instrument, which consists of seven (7) pages, including the pages on which the signature of KENNETH F. GOODALL and our signatures appear, to be the will of KENNETH F. GOODALL, we subscribe our names as witnesses thereto.

We declare under penalty of perjury under the laws of the State of California that the foregoing is true and correct. Executed on 8/24/94, at San Rafael, California.

James R. Hastings residing at 18 San Rafael Avenue
San Anselmo, California

Nancy Rodgers residing at 470 Peachstone Terrace
San Rafael, California 94903

Will

RECEIVED FOR SAFE KEEPING

NOV 17 1994

FROM J.R. Hastings

HOWARD HANSON
MARIN COUNTY CLERK

BY

D. ROSS

LAW OFFICE OF
J. R. HASTINGS
18 SAN RAFAEL AVENUE
SAN ANSELMO, CALIFORNIA 94960
(415) 459-6635

Exhibit Q

Purported Last Will of Rachel Goodall

LAST WILL OF

RACHEL A. GOODALL

I, RACHEL A. GOODALL, a resident of Marin County, California, declare that this is my will. I hereby revoke all my previous wills and codicils.

ARTICLE ONE

INTRODUCTORY PROVISIONS

1.1. Marital Status. I am married to KENNETH F. GOODALL, and all references in this will to "my husband" are to him.

1.2. Identification of Living Child. I have one living child, KENNETH MICHAEL GOODALL.

1.3. No Deceased Children. I have no deceased children.

ARTICLE TWO

RESIDUARY PROVISIONS

2.1. Disposition of Residue. I give the residue of my estate to the trustee of the GOODALL TRUST, created under the declaration of trust executed on September 12, 1990, by KENNETH F. GOODALL and RACHEL A. GOODALL, as Settlors and Trustees. The trustee of that trust shall add the residue of my estate to the trust principal and hold, administer, and distribute the property in accordance with the provisions of that declaration of trust, including any amendments of that declaration of trust that have been made before or after execution of this will.

2.2. Alternate Disposition of Residue. If the GOODALL TRUST has been revoked, terminated, or declared invalid for any reason, I give the portion of the residue of my estate not taken to the executor of this will, as trustee, who shall hold, administer, and distribute the property under a testamentary trust, the terms of which shall be identical to the terms of the GOODALL TRUST that are in effect on the date of execution of this will.

ARTICLE THREE

EXECUTOR

3.1. Nomination of Executors. I nominate my husband as executor of this will. If, for any reason, my husband fails to qualify or ceases to act as executor, I nominate BANK OF AMERICA, NT & SA, San Francisco, California, or any corporation that is a successor thereto by merger, consolidation, transfer of assets, or other manner provided by law, as executor of this will.

3.2. Waiver of Bond. No bond or undertaking shall be required of any executor nominated in this will.

3.3. General Powers of Executor. The executor shall have full authority to administer my estate under the California Independent Administration of Estates Act. The executor shall have all powers now or hereafter conferred on executors by law, except as otherwise specifically provided in this will, including any powers enumerated in this will.

3.4. Power to Invest. The executor shall have the power to

invest estate funds in any kind of real or personal property, as the executor deems advisable.

3.5. Division or Distribution in Cash or in Kind. In order to satisfy a pecuniary gift or to distribute or divide estate assets into shares or partial shares, the executor may distribute or divide those assets in kind, or divide undivided interests in those assets, or sell all or any part of those assets and distribute or divide the property in cash, in kind, or partly in cash and partly in kind. Property distributed to satisfy a pecuniary gift under this will shall be valued at its fair market value at the time of distribution.

3.6. Power to Sell, Lease, and Grant Options to Purchase Property. The executor shall have the power to sell, at either public or private sale and with or without notice, lease, and grant options to purchase any real or personal property belonging to my estate, on such terms and conditions as the executor determines to be in the best interest of my estate.

3.7. Power to Purchase Estate Property. The executor shall have the power to sell any property of my estate to, or exchange any property of my estate with the property of, my husband, even though he is also an executor at the time of the sale or exchange, provided that any such sale or exchange shall be for adequate consideration.

3.8. Payments to Legally Incapacitated Persons. If at any time any beneficiary under this will is a minor or it appears to the executor that any beneficiary is incapacitated, incompetent, or for any other reason not able to receive payments or make intelligent or responsible use of the payments, then the executor, in lieu of making direct payments to the beneficiary, may make payments to the beneficiary's conservator or guardian; to the beneficiary's custodian under the Uniform Gifts to Minors Act or Uniform Transfers to Minors Act of any state; to one or more suitable persons, as the executor deems proper, such as a relative or a person residing with the beneficiary, to be used for the benefit of the beneficiary; to any other person, firm, or agency for services rendered or to be rendered for the beneficiary's assistance or benefit; or to accounts in the beneficiary's name with financial institutions. The receipt of payments by any of the foregoing shall constitute a sufficient acquittance of the executor for all purposes.

ARTICLE FOUR

CONCLUDING PROVISIONS

4.1. Nonprobate Transfers of Community Property. If I predecease my husband, I revoke any consent I have given during my lifetime to any nonprobate transfer on the death of any person, to anyone other than my husband, of all or part of my community property interest in any asset described in California Probate Code Section 5000 (or any successor section), and instead I give to my husband my community property interest in any assets affected by this revocation of consent. Notwithstanding the preceding sentence, this revocation of consent shall be inapplicable to any community property included in any express trust of which I am the settlor or a cosettlor, which shall continue to be governed by the terms of the applicable trust instrument. It is my intention that my husband shall have full power to dispose of all community property assets to which this section of the will applies. If my husband and I die simultaneously or if it cannot be established by clear and convincing evidence whether my husband or I died first, this section shall not apply.

4.2. Definition of Death Taxes. The term "death taxes," as used in this will, shall mean all inheritance, estate, succession, and other similar taxes that are payable by any person on account of that person's interest in my estate or by reason of my death, including penalties and interest, but excluding the following:

(a) Any addition to the federal estate tax for any "excess retirement accumulation" under Internal Revenue Code Section 4980A.

(b) Any additional tax that may be assessed under Internal Revenue Code Section 2032A.

(c) Any federal or state tax imposed on a "generation-skipping transfer," as that term is defined in the federal tax laws, unless the applicable tax statutes provide that the generation-skipping transfer tax on that transfer is payable directly out of the assets of my gross estate.

4.3. Payment of Death Taxes. Pursuant to the declaration of trust executed on September 12, 1990, by KENNETH F. GOODALL and RACHEL A. GOODALL, as Settlors and Trustees, all death taxes, whether or not attributable to property inventoried in my probate estate, shall be paid by the trustee from that trust. However, if that trust does not exist at the time of my death, or if the assets of that trust are insufficient to pay the death taxes in full, I direct the executor to pay any death taxes that cannot be paid by the trustee from the assets of my probate estate by prorating and apportioning those taxes among the beneficiaries of this will, as provided in the California Probate Code.

4.4. Period of Survivorship. For the purposes of this will, a beneficiary shall not be deemed to have survived me if that beneficiary dies within forty (40) days after my death.

4.5. No-Contest Clause. If any person, directly or indirectly, contests the validity of this will in whole or in part, or opposes, objects to, or seeks to invalidate any of its provisions, or seeks to succeed to any part of my estate otherwise than in the manner specified in this will, any gift or other interest given to that person under this will shall be revoked and shall be disposed of as if he or she had predeceased me without issue.

4.6. Captions. The captions appearing in this will are for convenience of reference only, and shall be disregarded in determining the meaning and effect of the provisions of this will.

4.7. Severability Clause. If any provision of this will is invalid, that provision shall be disregarded, and the remainder of this will shall be construed as if the invalid provision had not been included.

4.8. California Law to Apply. All questions concerning the validity and interpretation of this will, including any trusts created by this will, shall be governed by the laws of the State of California in effect at the time this will is executed.

Executed on 8/24/94, at San Rafael, California.

Rachel A. Goodall
RACHEL A. GOODALL

On the date written above, we, the undersigned, each being present at the same time, witnessed the signing of this instrument by RACHEL A. GOODALL. At that time, RACHEL A. GOODALL appeared to us to be of sound mind and memory and, to the best of our knowledge, was not acting under fraud, duress, menace, or undue influence. Understanding this instrument, which consists of seven (7) pages, including the pages on which the signature of RACHEL A. GOODALL and our signatures appear, to be the will of RACHEL A. GOODALL, we subscribe our names as witnesses thereto.

We declare under penalty of perjury under the laws of the State of California that the foregoing is true and correct. Executed on 8/24/94, at San Rafael, California.

James R. Hastings residing at 18 San Rafael Avenue
San Anselmo, California

Nancy Rodgers residing at 470 Peachstone Terrace
San Rafael, California 94903

Exhibit R

Power of Attorney by Rachel Goodall given to Michael Goodall endorsed by Col. Kenneth Goodall

<u>DURABLE POWER OF ATTORNEY</u>

<u>FOR MANAGEMENT OF PROPERTY AND PERSONAL AFFAIRS</u>

I, RACHEL A. GOODALL, a resident of Marin County, California, appoint KENNETH F. GOODALL of 461 Peachstone Terrace, San Rafael, California 94903, whose telephone number is (415) 479-3599, as my attorney in fact. If KENNETH F. GOODALL dies, resigns, is unable to act because of incapacity, or is unwilling to act, I appoint KENNETH MICHAEL GOODALL as my attorney in fact. All references herein to "my attorney in fact" refer to the attorney in fact acting at the pertinent time.

I intend to create a Durable Power of Attorney (herein referred to as "this Power") pursuant to California Civil Code Section 2400 and following, but specifically not including Section 2430 and following relating to health care. This Power shall become effective upon my incapacity as determined in accordance with Paragraph 2.1 of this Power. If, after being determined incapacitated, I should regain my capacity as determined in accordance with Paragraph 2.2 of this Power, the powers granted to my attorney in fact in Article One and elsewhere in this Power shall cease.

I give my attorney in fact the powers specified in this Power with the understanding that they will be used for my benefit and on my behalf and will be exercised only in a fiduciary capacity.

ARTICLE ONE

POWERS

1.1. Real and Personal Property. I give my attorney in fact the power to take any actions he believes necessary or desirable for the management or maintenance of any real or personal property in which I own an interest when this Power is executed, including the real property specifically described in Exhibit A, or in which I later acquire an interest, including the power to acquire, sell, and convey ownership of property; control the manner in which property is managed, maintained, and used; change the form of title in which property is held; satisfy and grant security interests and other encumbrances on property; obtain and make claims on insurance policies covering risks of loss or damage to property; accept or remove tenants; collect proceeds generated by property; ensure that any needed repairs are made to property; exercise rights of participation in real estate syndicates or other real estate ventures; make improvements to property; and perform any other acts described in California Civil Code Sections 2486 and 2487, except those acts that conflict with or are limited by a more specific provision in this Power.

1.2. Securities. I give my attorney in fact the power to take any actions he believes necessary or desirable with respect to any securities that I own when this Power becomes effective, or that are acquired thereafter, including the power to purchase and sell securities; exercise voting rights with respect to securities; collect dividends, interest, and any other proceeds generated by securities; transfer title to securities; and perform any other acts described in California Civil Code Section 2488, except those acts that conflict with or are limited by a more specific provision in this Power. For the purposes of this paragraph, the term "securities" includes stocks, bonds, mutual funds, and all other types of securities and financial instruments, except commodity futures contracts and call and put options on stocks and stock indexes.

1.3. Financial Institutions. I give my attorney in fact the power to take any actions he believes necessary or desirable in connection with any financial institution in which I have an account or an interest in an account when this Power is executed, or in which I later acquire an account or an interest in an account, including the power to continue, modify, or terminate existing accounts; open new accounts; draw, endorse, and deposit checks, drafts, and other negotiable instruments; prepare, receive, and deliver financial statements; establish, maintain, or close safe deposit boxes; borrow money; apply for and receive travelers checks and letters of credit; extend payment periods with respect to commercial paper; and perform any other acts described in California Civil Code Section 2490, except those acts that conflict with or are limited by a more specific provision in this Power. For the purposes of this paragraph, the term "financial institution" includes, but is not limited to, banks, trust companies, savings banks, commercial banks, building and loan associations, savings and loan companies or associations, credit unions, industrial loan companies, thrift companies, and brokerage firms.

1.4. <u>Business Operations</u>. I give my attorney in fact the power to take any actions he believes necessary or desirable in connection with any business venture in which I have an interest when this Power is executed, or in which I later acquire an interest, including the power to execute and enforce my obligations and rights as a partner in any general or limited partnership to the extent permitted by law and any applicable partnership agreement; enforce my rights as the holder of a bond or similar instrument issued by any business in which I have an interest; discharge my duties and enforce my rights in any sole proprietorship; expand, recapitalize, or reorganize any business to the extent my interest in that business allows; collect proceeds generated by any business in which I have an interest and to which I am entitled; sell or liquidate my interest in a business; and perform any other acts described in California Civil Code Section 2491, except those acts that conflict with or are limited by a more specific provision in this Power.

1.5. <u>Insurance and Annuities</u>. I give my attorney in fact the power to take any actions he believes necessary or desirable with respect to any insurance or annuity contracts in which I have an interest when this Power is executed, or in which I later acquire an interest, including the power to acquire additional insurance coverage of any type or additional annuities; continue existing insurance or annuity contracts; agree to modifications in the terms of insurance or annuity contracts in which I have an interest; borrow against insurance or annuity contracts in which I have an interest, to the extent allowed under the contract terms; change beneficiaries under existing contracts and name beneficiaries under new contracts, including the power to designate himself as the beneficiary; receive dividends, proceeds, and other benefits generated by the contracts; transfer interests in insurance or annuity contracts to the extent permitted under the terms of those contracts; and perform any other acts described in California Civil Code Section 2492, except those acts that conflict with or are limited by a more specific provision in this Power.

1.6. Retirement Plans. I give my attorney in fact the power to take any actions he believes necessary or desirable in order to maintain or participate in any retirement plan in which I have an interest when this Power is executed, or in which I later acquire an interest, including the power to select the manner in which benefits under the plan are to be paid; designate beneficiaries under the plan, including the power to designate himself as the beneficiary; make voluntary contributions to the plan; make rollovers from one plan into another; to the extent authorized by the plan, borrow from the plan and sell the assets of the plan; and perform any other acts described in California Civil Code Section 2497, except those acts that conflict with or are limited by a more specific provision in this Power.

1.7. Estate, Trust, and Other Beneficiary Transactions. I give my attorney in fact the power to take any actions he believes necessary or desirable in order to act, to the extent an agent is permitted to do so by law and by any controlling instrument, with respect to any estate or trust in which I have an interest when this Power is executed, or in which I later acquire an interest, including the power to receive payments to which I am entitled from any estate or trust; participate in all proceedings concerning any estate or trust in which I have an interest; execute disclaimers of any interests I may have in any estate or trust; convey or release any contingent interests I may have in any estate or trust; make any election available to a surviving spouse under California Probate Code Section 13502 or 13503; and perform any other acts described in California Civil Code Section 2493, except those acts that conflict with or are limited by a more specific provision in this Power. For the purposes of this paragraph, the term "estate or trust" means all matters that affect a trust, probate estate, guardianship, conservatorship, escrow, custodianship, or other fund from which I am, may become, or claim to be entitled, as a beneficiary, to a share or payment. The powers described in this paragraph do not include the power to create, modify, or revoke trusts.

1.8. Power to Create, Modify, and Revoke Trusts. I give my attorney in fact the power to take any action he believes necessary or desirable with respect to trusts that exist when this Power is executed or that are established thereafter (other than powers that I hold in a fiduciary capacity or solely by virtue of being a beneficiary of any trust), including the power to establish trusts for my benefit or the benefit of my husband, my issue, and any other of my dependents; contribute or transfer assets to any trust in which I have an interest; and exercise any power I may have as an individual (not as a fiduciary), other than as a trust beneficiary, such as borrowing trust assets, amending or revoking a trust agreement, and voting shares of stock, but subject to the limitation that any trust I have created may be modified or revoked by my attorney in fact only if expressly permitted by the trust instrument. This paragraph shall not be construed as limiting the authority of my attorney in fact to exercise any power, with respect to trusts, that I may hold in a fiduciary capacity or as a trust beneficiary, to the extent that such authority is specifically given elsewhere in this Power.

1.9. Claims and Litigation. I give my attorney in fact the power to take any actions he believes necessary or desirable with respect to any claim that I may have or that has been asserted against me and with respect to any legal proceeding in which I have an interest when this Power is executed, or in which I later acquire an interest, including the power to institute, prosecute, and defend legal proceedings and claims on my behalf; file actions to determine adverse claims, intervene in litigation, and act as amicus curiae in any proceedings affecting my interests; seek preliminary, provisional, or intermediate relief on my behalf; apply for the enforcement or satisfaction of judgments that have been rendered in my favor; participate fully in the development of claims and proceedings; submit any dispute in which I have an interest to arbitration; submit and accept settlement offers and participate in settlement negotiations; handle all procedural aspects, such as service of process, filing of appeals, stipulations, verifications, waivers, and all other matters in any way affecting the process of any claim or litigation; fully participate in any voluntary or involuntary bankruptcy proceeding involving me or in which I am a claimant; satisfy judgments that have been rendered against me; and perform any other acts described in California Civil Code Section 2494, except those acts that conflict with or are limited by a more specific provision in this Power.

1.10. Tax Matters. I give my attorney in fact the power to prepare and file any and all documents and take all actions that are necessary or that he believes to be desirable with respect to my local, state, or federal tax liability, including the power to participate in audits; exercise my rights to protest and appeal assessments; pay amounts due to the appropriate taxing authority; execute waivers, consents, closing agreements, and similar documents related to my tax liability; participate in all procedural matters connected with my tax liability; exercise any elections that may be available to me under applicable state or federal tax laws or regulations; and perform any other acts described in California Civil Code Section 2498, except those acts that conflict with or are limited by a more specific provision in this Power.

1.11. Personal and Family Maintenance. I give my attorney in fact the power to take any actions he believes necessary or desirable in order to effectively conduct my personal affairs and to discharge any and all obligations I may owe to myself and to family members and other third persons who are customarily or legally entitled to my support when this Power is executed, or that are undertaken thereafter, including the power to take steps to ensure that our customary standard of living is maintained; arrange for medical and dental care; continue existing charge accounts, open new charge accounts, and make payments thereon; provide for transportation; maintain correspondence; prepare, maintain, and preserve personal records and documents; maintain membership in any social, religious, or professional organization and make contributions thereto; and perform any other acts described in California Civil Code Section 2495, except those acts that conflict with or are limited by a more specific provision in this Power.

1.12. Funeral and Burial. I give my attorney in fact the power to arrange for my funeral or other memorial service and for burial or cremation of my remains, including the purchase of a burial plot or other place for interment of my remains or ashes.

1.13. Gifts. I give my attorney in fact the power to make gifts, grants, or other transfers without consideration, of cash or other property, either outright or in trust, including the power to forgive indebtedness and consent to gift splitting under Internal Revenue Code Section 2513 or successor sections. The powers granted under this paragraph shall be exercised, if at all, in favor of my husband, my issue, and any other of my dependents. Any gifts made pursuant to this paragraph shall not be future interests within the meaning of Internal Revenue Code Section 2503, and the aggregate amount of any gifts made in any one calendar year to any one individual shall not exceed the amount that may be made free of federal gift tax to a person. The limitations in the preceding sentence shall not apply to any gifts that incur no federal gift tax, such as, for example, gifts that qualify for the unlimited federal gift tax marital deduction or charitable deduction.

1.14. Gifts to Attorney in Fact Limited to Ascertainable Standard. Notwithstanding any other provision in this Power, my attorney in fact may make gifts in amounts not to exceed the annual federal gift tax exclusion to himself, but only if he is in need of funds to meet the reasonable expenses of the following: (1) support in accordance with his accustomed manner of living; (2) medical, dental, hospital, and nursing services, and other costs relating to the health care of my attorney in fact; and (3) education of my attorney in fact.

1.15. Government Benefits. With respect to any government benefits either existing when this Power is executed or accruing thereafter, whether in this state or elsewhere, I give my attorney in fact the power to take all actions he believes necessary or desirable, including the power to execute and deliver vouchers related to government benefits; take possession of and store property as allowed under any government benefit program in which I have an interest; prepare and submit claims for government benefits to which I may be entitled; collect proceeds due to me under any government benefit plan; and perform any other acts described in California Civil Code Section 2496, except those acts that conflict with or are limited by a more specific provision in this Power. For the purposes of this paragraph, the term "government benefits" means benefits from social security, medicare, medicaid, or other governmental programs, or from civil or military service.

1.16. Nomination of Conservator. If proceedings are initiated for the appointment of a conservator of my person or my estate or both, I hereby nominate the attorney in fact then serving as conservator of my person, estate, or person and estate. I hereby waive the requirement of a bond for this conservator. I request that, if the person named above is appointed conservator of my estate, the court make an order granting to that person all or as many of those independent powers listed in California Probate Code Section 2591 as the court deems appropriate.

1.17. All Other Matters. Except for those actions that conflict with or are limited by another provision in this Power, I give my attorney in fact the power to act as my alter ego with respect to all matters and affairs that are not included in the other provisions in this Power, to the extent that a principal can act through an agent. This paragraph does not authorize my attorney in fact to make health care decisions, as defined in California Civil Code Section 2430.

1.18. Incidental Powers. In connection with the exercise of any of the powers described in the preceding paragraphs, I give my attorney in fact full authority, to the extent that a principal can act through an agent, to take all actions that he believes necessary, proper, or convenient, to the extent that I could take such actions myself, including the power to prepare, execute, and file all documents and maintain records; enter into contracts; hire, discharge, and pay reasonable compensation to attorneys, accountants, expert witnesses, or other assistants; engage in litigation regarding a claim in favor of or against me; execute, acknowledge, seal, and deliver any instrument; and perform any other acts described in California Civil Code Section 2485, except those acts that conflict with or are limited by a more specific provision in this Power.

ARTICLE TWO

AMPLIFYING PROVISIONS

2.1. Determination of Incapacity. For all purposes under this Power, I shall be deemed "incapacitated" if and so long as a court of competent jurisdiction has made a finding to that effect or a guardian or conservator of my person or estate duly appointed by a court of competent jurisdiction is serving, or upon certification by two physicians (licensed to practice under the laws of the state where I am domiciled at the time of the certification) that I am unable properly to care for myself or for my person or property, which certification shall be made by each physician in a written declaration under penalty of perjury. A certified copy of the decree declaring incapacity or appointing a guardian or conservator, or the physicians' certificate shall be attached to the original of this document and recorded in the same county or counties as the original if the original is recorded.

2.2. Capacity Regained. After a determination of incapacity, I shall be deemed to have regained capacity by a finding of a court of competent jurisdiction to that effect, or when the guardianship or conservatorship for me has been judicially terminated, or upon certification by two physicians (licensed to practice under the laws of the state where I am domiciled at the time of the certification) that I am capable of properly caring for myself or am able to manage my person or property, which certification shall be made by each physician in a written declaration under penalty of perjury. A certified copy of the decree declaring my regained capacity or terminating the guardianship or conservatorship, or the physicians' certificate, shall be attached to the original of this document and recorded in the same county or counties as the original if the original is recorded.

2.3. Reimbursement for Costs and Expenses. My attorney in

fact shall be entitled to reimbursement from my property for expenditures properly made in the execution of the powers conferred by me in this Power. My attorney in fact shall keep records of any such expenditures and reimbursement.

2.4. Reasonable Compensation. My attorney in fact shall be entitled to reasonable compensation for the services rendered in the execution of any of the powers conferred in this Power. In determining the reasonableness of compensation, all relevant factors shall be taken into consideration, including, but not limited to, the time expended by my attorney in fact, the value of the property over which my attorney in fact exercises control and management, and the complexity of the transactions entered into by my attorney in fact. My attorney in fact may make the payment of such amount from my assets every month. My attorney in fact shall keep records that include the amount of time spent in performing the services, a description of the services performed, and the amount of compensation paid to himself for each such time period.

2.5. Reliance by Third Parties. To induce third parties to rely upon the provisions of this Power, I, for myself and on behalf of my heirs, successors, and assigns, hereby waive any privilege that may attach to information requested by my attorney in fact in the exercise of any of the powers described herein. Moreover, on behalf of my heirs, successors, and assigns, I hereby agree to hold harmless any third party who acts in reliance upon this Power for damages or liability incurred as a result of that reliance.

2.6. Release of Medical Information. I authorize in advance all providers of health care, including hospitals, to release to my attorney in fact all information or photocopies of any records that my attorney in fact requests. If I am able to confirm this authorization at the time of the request, third parties may seek such confirmation from me, but this authorization shall not be conditional on my confirmation. All providers of health care shall treat the request of my attorney in fact as that of a legal representative of an incompetent patient, as contemplated by California Civil Code Section 56.11(c)(2), or any successor section, and shall honor that request on such a basis. I hereby waive any privilege applicable to such information and records, and to any communication pertaining to me and made in the course of a physician-patient or psychiatrist-patient relationship, and I hold the provider of health care harmless for any liability for the release of such information.

2.7. Ratification. I ratify and confirm all that my attorney in fact does or causes to be done under the authority granted in this Power. All instruments of any sort entered into in any manner by my attorney in fact shall bind me, my estate, my heirs, successors, and assigns.

2.8. Exculpation of My Attorney in Fact. My attorney in fact shall not be liable to me or any of my successors in interest for any action taken or not taken in good faith, but shall be liable for any willful misconduct or gross negligence.

2.9. Revocation and Amendment. I revoke all prior General Powers of Attorney that I may have executed and I retain the right to revoke or amend this document and to substitute other attorneys in fact in place of my attorney in fact. Amendments to this document shall be made in writing by me personally (not by my attorney in fact) and they shall be attached to the original of this document and recorded in the same county or counties as the original if the original is recorded.

2.10. Power to Petition Court. I expressly eliminate, pursuant to California Civil Code Section 2421, the authority of all persons except the attorney in fact then serving and me to file a petition for the following purposes:

(a) To determine whether this power is in effect or has terminated.

(b) To request that the court pass on the acts or the proposed acts of my attorney in fact.

(c) To compel my attorney in fact to submit accounts.

(d) To request that the court declare this power terminated.

ARTICLE THREE

GENERAL PROVISIONS

3.1. Signature of Attorney in Fact. My attorney in fact shall use the following form when signing on my behalf pursuant to this Power: "RACHEL A. GOODALL by (name of attorney in fact), her attorney in fact."

3.2. Photostatic Copies. Persons dealing with my attorney

in fact may not rely fully on a photostatic copy of this Power.

3.3. Severability. If any of the provisions of this Power are found to be invalid for any reason, such invalidity shall not affect any of the other provisions of this Power, and all invalid provisions shall be wholly disregarded.

3.4. Governing Law. All questions pertaining to validity, interpretation, and administration of this Power shall be determined in accordance with the laws of California.

3.5. Explanation of Durable Power for Property Management. I understand that this Power is an important legal document. Before executing this document, my lawyer explained to me the following: (1) this document provides my attorney in fact with broad powers to dispose of, sell, convey, and encumber my real and personal property; (2) the powers granted in this Power will exist for an indefinite period of time unless I limit their duration by the terms of this Power or revoke this Power, and they will continue to exist notwithstanding my subsequent disability or incapacity; and (3) I have the right to revoke or terminate this Power at any time.

This Durable Power of Attorney is executed by me on 5/4/94 at San Rafael, California.

Rachel A. Goodall

RACHEL A. GOODALL

Acceptance by Attorney in Fact

Kenneth F. Goodall

KENNETH F. GOODALL

Dated: 5/4/94

ACKNOWLEDGMENT

STATE OF CALIFORNIA)
) ss
COUNTY OF MARIN)

On 5/24/94, before me, James R. Hastings, notary public, personally appeared RACHEL A. GOODALL, personally known to me (or proved to me on the basis of satisfactory evidence) to be the person whose name is subscribed to the within instrument and acknowledged to me that she executed the same in her authorized capacity, and that by her signature on the instrument the person, or the entity upon behalf of which the person acted, executed the instrument.

WITNESS my hand and official seal.

Signature ______________________

(SEAL) JAMES R. HASTINGS COMM. #997773 NOTARY PUBLIC-CALIFORNIA MARIN COUNTY My Comm. Expires Aug. 20, 1997

LAWYER'S CERTIFICATE

I am a lawyer authorized to practice law in the state where this power of attorney was executed, and the principal was my client at the time this power of attorney was executed. I have advised my client concerning her rights in connection with this power of attorney and the applicable law and the consequences of signing or not signing this power of attorney, and my client, after being so advised, has executed this power of attorney.

Dated: ______________

____
James R. Hastings

Law Firm: Law Office of James R. Hastings
Address: 18 San Rafael Avenue, San Anselmo, California 94960
Telephone Number: (415) 459-6635

STATEMENT OF RACHEL A. GOODALL

I, RACHEL A. GOODALL, am the principal under a Durable Power of Attorney for Property Management and Personal Affairs, which was prepared for me by James R. Hastings and which I am executing at the same time that I am executing this statement. I hereby acknowledge that James R. Hastings advised me fully concerning my rights in connection with this Durable Power of Attorney for Property Management and Personal Affairs and explained the applicable law and the consequences of signing or not signing this Durable Power of Attorney for Property Management and Personal Affairs. I have been shown and have read the warnings contained in subdivision (b) of California Civil Code Section 2510, a copy of which is attached hereto and which I have initialed.

Executed on ____________________, at San Rafael, California.

RACHEL A. GOODALL

California Civil Code Section 2510 (b)

WARNING TO PERSON EXECUTING THIS DOCUMENT

THIS IS AN IMPORTANT LEGAL DOCUMENT. IT CREATES A DURABLE POWER OF ATTORNEY. BEFORE EXECUTING THIS DOCUMENT, YOU SHOULD KNOW THESE IMPORTANT FACTS:

THIS DOCUMENT MAY PROVIDE THE PERSON YOU DESIGNATE AS YOUR ATTORNEY IN FACT WITH BROAD POWERS TO MANAGE, DISPOSE, SELL, AND CONVEY YOUR REAL AND PERSONAL PROPERTY AND TO BORROW MONEY USING YOUR PROPERTY AS SECURITY FOR THE LOAN.

THESE POWERS WILL EXIST FOR AN INDEFINITE PERIOD OF TIME UNLESS YOU LIMIT THEIR DURATION IN THIS DOCUMENT. THESE POWERS WILL CONTINUE TO EXIST NOTWITHSTANDING YOUR SUBSEQUENT DISABILITY OR INCAPACITY.

YOU HAVE THE RIGHT TO REVOKE OR TERMINATE THIS POWER OF ATTORNEY.

IF THERE IS ANYTHING ABOUT THIS FORM THAT YOU DO NOT UNDERSTAND, YOU SHOULD ASK A LAWYER TO EXPLAIN IT TO YOU.

____

Initials

EXHIBIT A

The following described real property in the City of San Rafael, County of Marin, State of California:

> Lot No. 1068, "Map of Marinwood Unit 7", County of Marin, Initially recorded 19 Oct. 1959 in Map Book #10, Page 42, Marin County Records.

Exhibit S

Declaration filed by James R. Hastings in San Francisco Probate Court stating among other things that he is the attorney for all parties on both sides of this case

Don A. Lesser (SBN #112887)
THE LESSER LAW GROUP
1010 B Street, Suite 300
San Rafael, California 94901
Telephone: (415) 453-7600
Facsimile: (415) 295-4122
E-mail: DLesser@LesserGroup.com

Attorney for Subpoenaed Witness
JAMES R. HASTINGS

FILED
SUPERIOR COURT
COUNTY OF SAN FRANCISCO

2012 FEB -2 PM 3:26

CLERK OF THE COURT
BY: [signature]
DEPUTY CLERK

CALIFORNIA SUPERIOR COURT

SAN FRANCISCO COUNTY

In the Matter of the Trust for Michael created under the Goodall Trust dated January 19, 1999	Case No. PTR-99-273030 **DECLARATION OF JAMES R. HASTINGS PURSUANT TO COURT ORDER ON RESPONDENT'S MOTION TO COMPEL PRODUCTION OF DOCUMENTS AND FURTHER DEPOSITION** Hearing: January 12, 2012 Time: 2:15 p.m. Department: 204

BY FAX

I, James R. Hastings, declare as follows:

1. I am an attorney at law licensed to practice in the State of California. I provide this declaration in response to this Court's order on Respondent's Motion to Compel Production of Documents and Further Deposition. The following facts are personally known to me. If called upon to do so, I could and would testify competently to them.

2. This declaration describes my further search for my Estate Planning file relating to Kenneth and Rachel Goodall, following my November 14, 2011 deposition in this matter. Since then, I have re-examined the two groups of files I have at my home. As the number of the file I

am looking for begins with the letter "G," I looked at every "G" file in those files at my home and did not find the Goodalls' file. I also looked in both storage areas at my office, active and inactive, again looking at every "G" file, and again found nothing. I also looked at all of the Goodall files retained in an armoire near my assistant's work area, which contains "active" files. I then looked at *all* of the files in that armoire, and still found nothing. I have searched my entire office, where I prepared the declarations I have submitted in this matter. Previously I inquired of all the staff people who work in my office when and where they last saw the file, and no one could recall.

3. I have not knowingly discarded or destroyed the file, or instructed anyone else to do so, nor have I knowingly given it to anyone else. At this point, I have searched everywhere I can think of where the file might be found.

I declare under penalty of perjury under the laws of the State of California that the foregoing is true and correct and that this declaration was executed this 1 day of February, 2012 at San Rafael, California.

James R. Hastings

PROOF OF SERVICE

I, the undersigned, declare: I am over the age of 18 years at the time of service, and am not a party to the within action. I am employed in the County of Marin. My business address is 1010 B Street, Suite 350, San Rafael, California 94901.

On this date, February 2, 2012, the following document(s) were served:

DECLARATION OF JAMES R. HASTINGS PURSUANT TO COURT ORDER ON RESPONDENT'S MOTION TO COMPEL PRODUCTION OF DOCUMENTS AND FURTHER DEPOSITION

on the parties, through their attorneys of record, by means of service designated below:

Samuel G. Ware 700 Larkspur Landing Circle Suite 199 Larkspur, CA 94939	**(By First Class Mail)** I caused each such envelope, with first-class postage thereon fully prepaid, to be deposited in the United States mail at San Rafael, California.
John L. McDonnell, Jr. Reed Smith LLP 1999 Harrison Street, 24th Floor Oakland, CA 94612	**(By First Class Mail)** I caused each such envelope, with first-class postage thereon fully prepaid, to be deposited in the United States mail at San Rafael, California.
Gary D. Rothstein Manat Phelps Phillips One Embarcadero Center, 30th Fl. San Francisco, CA 94111	**(By First Class Mail)** I caused each such envelope, with first-class postage thereon fully prepaid, to be deposited in the United States mail at San Rafael, California.

I declare under penalty of perjury that the foregoing is true and correct and that this Declaration was executed on February 2, 2012, at San Rafael, California.

Gina Anthony

GINA ANTHONY

James R. Hastings (SBN 079066)
J. R. HASTINGS LAW CORPORATION
1003 Third Street
San Rafael, CA 94901-3107
(415) 459-6635 (tel)
(415) 459-6756 (fax)

Attorney for ROY HOPPE and
FRANK THORNALLY

FILED
SUPERIOR COURT
COUNTY OF SAN FRANCISCO
2011 AUG 19 AM 11:57
CLERK OF THE COURT
BY: [signature]
DEPUTY CLERK

FILED BY FAX

SUPERIOR COURT OF CALIFORNIA

COUNTY OF SAN FRANCISCO

In the Matter of the Trust for Michael created under the Goodall Trust dated September 12, 1990.	CASE NO. PTR-99-273030 **DECLARATION OF JAMES R. HASTINGS FAMILY AND ESTATE PLANNING ATTORNEY FOR THE GOODALLS** Hearing: August 22, 2011 Time: 9:00 a.m. Dept.: Probate, Rm. 204

I, JAMES R. HASTINGS, declare as follows:

1. I am an attorney licensed to practice law in the States of California, Colorado, Nevada and the District of Columbia. I am the principal in the LAW OFFICE OF J.R. HASTINGS. Except as otherwise stated, I have personal knowledge of the matter stated herein, if called and sworn as a witness could and would testify.

2. I was the family and estate planning counsel of Kenneth F. Goodall, from on or about August of 1990 until his death on September 10, 1994. I was the family and estate planning counsel for Rachel A. Goodall from on or about August of 1990 until her death on June 7, 1999. I was the trust administration attorney for the Trust Department of the Bank of America from on or about July 19, 1999 through on or about December of 2000. I was the family and estate planning counsel for the son of

Kenneth F. Goodall and Rachel A. Goodall, K. Michael Goodall, from on or about July of 1999 until his death on October 5 of 2010. Regarding the Last Will of K. Michael Goodall, dated January 15, 2004, I was the estate attorney for the named executors Ray Hoppe and Frank Thornally from on or about October of 2010 until on or about January 2011.

3. I will present a chronology in this declaration, but before I do so I state that these are truths which may be pertinent to the issues before the court:

a. On their own volition, Kenneth F. Goodall and Rachel A. Goodall chose Guide Dogs for the Blind in San Rafael, California, as the residuary beneficiary of their estate. K. Michael Goodall understood he had no right to the residuary estate of Kenneth F. Goodall and Rachel A. Goodall, and he understood that he had no power to direct the residuary benefits of their estate.

b. I did not, nor has anyone in my employ, ever received or had an agreement with Guide Dogs for the Blind for any remuneration resulting from the fact that Kenneth F. Goodall and Rachel A. Goodall named Guide Dogs for the Blind as a residuary beneficiary. Further, there has not been nor is there any agreement for any remuneration in the past, in the present or in the future.

c. The operative document defining the distribution of the estate of Kenneth F. Goodall and the operative document defining the distribution of the estate of Rachel A. Goodall is the Declaration of the Goodall Trust dated August 24, 1994, an amended and restated declaration of the original trust dated September 12, 1990. Accordingly, this amended and restated declaration replaced in its entirety the declaration of September 12, 1990; however, the trust retains the original date, though it had been amended and restated.

4. I first met Kenneth F. Goodall on or about 1980 as I employed him to make door signs for my office. After his retirement as a Lieutenant Colonel in the United States Air Force, Kenneth F. Goodall established a sign making business out of his garage. Subsequently, I met Rachel A. Goodall, a homemaker. Mr. and Mrs. Goodall were very honorable, religious, good and wonderful people.

5. Kenneth F. Goodall and Rachel A. Goodall had one son, J. Michael Goodall, born approximately 1950. K. Michael Goodall was gifted in many ways, including being a chess master. Unfortunately, his parents found him subject to the undue influence of others, resulting in caution in their ultimate estate plan.

6. On or about August 1990, after employing Kenneth F. Goodall to make signs for me, Kenneth F. Goodall and Rachel A. Goodall visited me for estate planning advice and preparation. During the estate planning consultations with Mr. and Mrs. Goodall, they directed me as to their desires for the disposition of their estate. These desires were reflected in the document entitled the Goodall Trust, which was signed by Kenneth F. Goodall and Rachel A. Goodall, their signatures notarized by me, on September 12, 1990. Though the document speaks for itself, after the first death this declaration contemplated the estate being divided into two parts, one part for the survivor, a Survivor's Trust, and one part representing the deceased's estate, a Credit Shelter Trust. The document provided at paragraph 6.3(a) that the residuary beneficiary of both of those trusts would be K. Michael Goodall, if living, and if

not, paragraph 6.3(b) gave gifts to family members and the residual estate to Guide Dogs for the Blind.

7. On or about late July or early August of 1994, Kenneth F. Goodall and Rachel A. Goodall again visited me for advice and document preparation concerning their estate plan. During the discussions they told me of the changes they wished to make to their estate plan. Those changes were recorded in the amended and restated declaration of trust dated August 24, 1994, a document signed by them, of which I acted as the Notary Public. This document retained the division of the estate at the first death, creating a Survivor's Trust and a Bypass ("Credit Shelter") Trust. The document revised the gift in paragraph 6.3(a) from a direct gift to their son, K. Michael Goodall, to a gift of a lifetime trust for K. Michael Goodall, this trust memorialized in Section 6.5. As indicated in a separate declaration signed by me and filed in this court, the Goodalls intended the ultimate distribution of the Trust for Michael to be the residuary beneficiary named in 6.3(b), Guide Dogs for the Blind. (Please see the attached Exhibit A.)

8. At no time did I suggest that the Guide Dogs for the Blind as the residuary beneficiary for the Goodalls; instead, the selection of Guide Dogs for the Blind as residuary beneficiary was communicated to me by them.

9. At no time have I received any remuneration for the fact that the Guide Dogs for the Blind is named as a residuary beneficiary in the trust declarations for the Goodalls. Neither has my staff. There has not been, is not now and will not be in the future any agreement for

remuneration from the Guide Dogs for the Blind for assisting the Goodalls to name them in their trust documents.

10. Kenneth F. Goodall died on September 10, 1994. When he died the declaration of the Goodall Trust dated August 24, 1994 was the operative document used for the trust administration of his estate. Similarly, the Last Will of Kenneth F. Goodall dated August 24, 1994, was lodged with the Clerk of the Court of Marin County, the distribution of this Last Will being a pour-over to the Goodall Trust dated August 24, 1994. During the subsequent trust administration several investment accounts were transferred to the Bypass Trust of the Goodall Trust, and the remainder of the assets, including the family home at 461 Peachstone Terrace, San Rafael, California, remained in the Goodall Trust as the Survivor's Trust. A Trustee's Deed transferring 461 Peachstone Terrace to the Survivor's Trust of the Goodall Trust was signed on June 8, 1995 and recorded on September 11, 1995 by the Marin County Recorder on September 11, 1995, as Document No. 95-042772.

11. Rachel A. Goodall died on June 7, 1999. When she died the Declaration of the Goodall Trust dated August 24, 1994 was the operative document used for the trust administration of her estate. Similarly, the Last Will of Rachel A. Goodall dated August 24, 1994, was lodged with the Clerk of the Court of Marin County, the distribution of this Last Will being a pour-over to the Goodall Trust dated August 24, 1994.

12. During the trust administration of the Estate of Rachel A. Goodall all assets of the Bypass Trust and the Survivor's Trust were passed to Bank of America, as trustee, and placed into the Trust for Michael as directed by the Declaration of Trust dated August 24, 1994. As a part

of that distribution a Notice Regarding Real Property, Affidavit of Death of Trustee and Acceptance of Office of Successor Trustee dated July 15, 1999, was recorded by the Marin County Recorder on October 26 of 2000. This document transferred the trusteeship and the ownership of 461 Peachstone Terrace, San Rafael, California, to the Bank of America Trust Department.

13. On or about July of 1999 K. Michael Goodall visited me for advice and documents concerning his estate plan. During that visit K. Michael Goodall informed me that he had no children, had not had any marriages and that his assets included personal property, his automobile and a bank account. The primary operative documents for K. Michael Goodall's estate plan were the Advance Health Care Directive and the Power of Attorney for Asset Management, documents assisting him should he become incapacitated. A will was completed, though K. Michael Goodall understood he did not have any assets which would ever require a probate, to ensure personal property and his minimal bank account would be properly handled at his passing.

14. Subsequently, I handled several general matters for K. Michael Goodall, including questions concerning his debts, problems with his license through the Department of Motor Vehicles, questions concerning debt relief and transmission of his Advance Health Care Directive to medical authorities during emergencies. Subsequently, as well, K. Michael Goodall revisited me on or about December of 2003 or early January of 2004 and refreshed all of his documents, which were the Advance Health Care Directive, property power of attorney and Last Will. In the Last Will he named two friends, Roy Hoppe and Frank Thornally, as

initial executors, and Bank of America as the subsequent executor. During our discussions and at the signing of both of his Last Wills, I clearly understood that K. Michael Goodall understood he has no residuary interest or power of appointment in the estate of his parents as comprised of the Trust for Michael of the Goodall Trust, the trust managed by the Bank of America following the death of his mother.

I declare under penalty of perjury that the foregoing declaration is true and correct and I executed same on August 18, 2011 at San Rafael, California.

Dated: August 18, 2011

JAMES R. HASTINGS, Declarant

EXHIBIT A

MANATT, PHELPS & PHILLIPS, LLP
GARY D. ROTHSTEIN (Bar No. CA 143157)
SUZANNE C. FARLEY (Bar No. CA 256693)
One Embarcadero Center, 30th Floor
San Francisco, CA 94111
Telephone: (415) 291-7400
Facsimile: (415) 291-7474

Attorneys for Petitioner,
BANK OF AMERICA, N.A.

SUPERIOR COURT OF THE STATE OF CALIFORNIA

FOR THE COUNTY OF SAN FRANCISCO

In the Matter of the Trust for Michael created under the Goodall Trust dated January 19, 1999.	Case No. **DECLARATION IN SUPPORT OF PETITION FOR DETERMINATION OF THE BENEFICIARIES TO WHOM TRUST PROPERTY SHALL PASS UPON TERMINATION OF TRUST** Hearing Date: Time: Dept.:

I, James Raymond Hastings, hereby declare as follows:

1. I am an active member of the State Bar of California and the principal in the Law Offices of J. R. Hastings. Except as otherwise stated, I have personal knowledge of the matters stated herein, and if called and sworn as a witness could and would testify competently thereto.

2. Bank of America, N.A. has filed a Petition for Determination of the Beneficiaries to Whom Trust Property Shall Pass Upon Termination of Trust (the "Petition"), in this matter.

3. I was estate planning counsel for Kenneth F. Goodall ("Kenneth") and Rachel A. Goodall ("Rachel") in connection with the Goodall Trust. I was responsible for the drafting of the Amendment to Goodall Trust dated August 24, 1994, and the Second Amendment

to Goodall Trust dated January 19, 1999 (collectively, the "Amendments").

4. In connection with the preparation of the Amendments, I discussed with Kenneth and Rachel how they wanted to dispose of the Goodall Trust estate upon their deaths and the death of their only child, Michael. It was my understanding based on that discussion that Rachel and Kenneth intended the balance of the trust established for the benefit of Michael ("the Trust for Michael") remaining at Michael's death to be distributed pursuant to Section 6.3(d) of the Goodall Trust, as follows: twenty thousand dollars to each of Rachel's then-living brothers and sisters, and the remainder to Guide Dogs for the Blind of Marin. Section 6.3(e) of the Goodall Trust, which states that the assets should be distributed one-half to Kenneth's heirs and one-half to Rachel's heirs, was intended to apply only if upon Michael's death there were no beneficiaries to take under Section 6.3(d) of the Goodall Trust.

5. The Petition seeks an order to determine the proper beneficiaries of the Trust for Michael in light of Michael's death and the resulting termination of the Trust for Michael. I have reviewed said Petition and believe that the determination sought by the Petition accurately reflects the intentions of Kenneth and Rachel.

I declare under penalty of perjury under the Laws of the State of California that the foregoing is true and correct.

Executed at San Rafael, California, on January 10 ~~xxx~~ ~~2010~~. 2011.

By: ______________________
James Raymond Hastings

300192417.2

MANATT, PHELPS & PHILLIPS, LLP
ATTORNEYS AT LAW
SAN FRANCISCO

ATTORNEY OR PARTY WITHOUT ATTORNEY (Name, State Bar number, and address):	FOR COURT USE ONLY
JAMES R. HASTINGS (SBN 079066) J.R. HASTINGS LAW CORPORATION 1003 THIRD STREET SAN RAFAEL, CA 94901-3107 TELEPHONE NO.: (415) 459-6635 FAX NO. (Optional): (415) 459-6756 E-MAIL ADDRESS (Optional): jrhastings@pacbell.net ATTORNEY FOR (Name): ROY HOPPE AND FRANK THORNALLY	
SUPERIOR COURT OF CALIFORNIA, COUNTY OF SAN FRANCISCO STREET ADDRESS: 400 McALLISTER STREET, RM 204 MAILING ADDRESS: CITY AND ZIP CODE: SAN FRANCISCO, CA 94102-4514 BRANCH NAME: PROBATE	
PLAINTIFF/PETITIONER: IN THE MATTER OF GOODALL TRUST	CASE NUMBER: PTR-99-273030
DEFENDANT/RESPONDENT:	JUDICIAL OFFICER:
PROOF OF ELECTRONIC SERVICE	DEPT.: PROBATE

1. I am at least 18 years old and **not a party to this action.**

   a. My residence or business address is *(specify)*:
   1003 THIRD STREET
   SAN RAFAEL, CA 94901-3107

   b. My electronic service address is *(specify)*:
   jrhastings@pacbell.net

2. I electronically served the following documents *(exact titles)*:
   DECLARATION OF JAMES R. HASTINGS FAMILY AND ESTATE PLANNING ATTORNEY FOR THE GOODALLS

   ☐ The documents served are listed in an attachment. *(Form POS-050(D)/EFS-050(D) may be used for this purpose.)*

3. I electronically served the documents listed in 2 as follows:

   a. Name of person served: SAM H. SLOAN
   On behalf of *(name or names of parties represented, if person served is an attorney)*:

   b. Electronic service address of person served: SAMHSLOAN@GMAIL.COM

   c. On *(date)*: AUGUST 19, 2011

   d. At *(time)*: 10:00 AM

   ☐ The documents listed in item 2 were served electronically on the persons and in the manner described in an attachment. *(Form POS-050(P)/EFS-050(P) may be used for this purpose.)*

Date: AUGUST 19, 2011

I declare under penalty of perjury under the laws of the State of California that the foregoing is true and correct.

RENEE MOORE ▶ Renee Moore

(TYPE OR PRINT NAME OF DECLARANT) (SIGNATURE OF DECLARANT)

Form Approved for Optional Use
Judicial Council of California
POS-050/EFS-050 [Rev. January 1, 2011]

PROOF OF ELECTRONIC SERVICE
(Proof of Service/Electronic Filing and Service)

Cal. Rules of Court, rule 2.251
www.courts.ca.gov

GOODALL

James R. Hastings, Esq. (SBN 079066)
J. R. HASTINGS LAW CORPORATION
1003 Third Street
San Rafael, CA 94901-3107
(415) 459-6635 (tel)
(415) 459-6756 (fax)

Attorney for
ROY HOPPE AND FRANK THORNALLY

SUPERIOR COURT OF CALIFORNIA

COUNTY OF SAN FRANCISCO

In The Matter of the Trust for Michael created Under the Goodall Trust dated January 19, 1999	CASE NO. PTR-99-273030 PROOF OF SERVICE

--SEE ATTACHED--

PROOF OF TRANSMISSION BY FAX
(California Rules of Court, rule 2.304)

In re the Matter of the Trust for Michael Created Under the Goodall Trust dated January 19, 1999

At the time of transmission, I was at least 18 years of age and not a party to this action. I am a resident of or employed in the county where the mailing occurred. My business address 1003 Third Street, San Rafael, CA 94901. On August 19, 2011 at 9:45AM I transmitted the within

DECLARATION OF JAMES R. HASTINGS, FAMILY AND ESTATE PLANNING ATTORNEY FOR THE GOODALLS

on each person named below by fax machine, under California Rules of Court, rule 2.304. The fax machine I used complied with California Rules of Court, rule 2.301 and no error was reported by the machine. Under California Rules of Court, rule 2.304, I caused the machine to print a record of the transmission, a copy of which is attached to this declaration. enclosing a copy in an envelope addressed as shown below and depositing the sealed envelope with the United States Postal Service on **August 19, 2011**, at San Rafael, California:

GARY D. ROTHSTEIN, ESQ.
MANATT, PHELPS & PHILLIPS, LLP
ONE EMBARCADERO AVENUE, 30TH FLOOR
SAN FRANCISCO, CA 94111
FAX NO: (415) 291-7474

I declare under penalty of perjury under the laws of the State of California that the foregoing is true and correct.

Dated: **August 19, 2011**

Renee Moore

TRANSMIT CONFIRMATION REPORT

NO.	:	003
RECEIVER	:	415 291 7474
TRANSMITTER	:	J. R. HASTINGS CORP.
DATE	:	AUG 19'11 9:43
DURATION	:	05'43
MODE	:	STD
PAGES	:	12
RESULT	:	OK

Exhibit T

Purported Signatures of the Kenneth and Rachel Goodall from the FAX produced by Bank of America on top compared with known actual signatures of Kenneth and Rachel Goodall on bottom from the same date. Note that in the real signatures Kenneth and Rachel Goodall used a light blue pen but the FAX supposedly from the same time and date is in heavy black ink.

Here is a comparison of the signatures between the known signatures of Kenneth and Rachel Goodall and the signatures on what purports to be the 1994 Trust

First, here are the signatures on what purports to be the trust document dated August 24, 1994.

Executed on ____5/24/94____ at San Rafael, California.

SETTLORS-TRUSTEES

Kenneth F. Goodall
KENNETH F. GOODALL

Rachel A. Goodall
RACHEL A. GOODALL

Now here are their known signatures bearing the same date of August 24, 1994 on the durable power of attorney in favor of their son Mike.

This Durable Power of Attorney is executed by me on

________________at San Rafael, California.

RACHEL A. GOODALL

Acceptance by Attorney in Fact

KENNETH F. GOODALL

Dated:________________

Please look especially at the letters F and G in the signature of Kenneth F. Goodall. This is the first thing the forensic document examiner David S. Moore noticed. The signature on the F followed by the G is made in one continuous non-stopping movement. First the top of the F is formed and then the pen loops around to make the G. The pen never leaves the paper.

However, in the trust document, the movement of the hand is shaky. The bottom of the F and then the G is formed and then the pen leaves the paper and comes back to make the top of the F as a straight line from right to left.

In the various documents and records signed over a period of years that we have, Kenneth F. Goodall signed his name as in the bottom signature every time. He never signed his name in the shaky halting way he supposedly signed the top signature here.

Several additional differences between the top and bottom signatures are plainly obvious. You do not have to be a forensic document examiner or any kind of expert to see them. It also appears that the documents were signed with a different pen, which is odd since they were both supposedly signed at the same time on the same date and place.

Exhibit U

Blowups of the Letters FG from the known signatures of Kenneth F. Goodall compared with the purported signature from the FAX. In the known signatures of Kenneth Goodall he signs the FG together with one stroke of the pen. However, in the trust document the top of the F is a different stroke right to left.

Using Adobe Photoshop to enlarge the signatures, here is a comparison between the FG in the signature of Kenneth F. Goodall on the Power of Attorney giving Kenneth Michael Goodall power of attorney in the event of the imminent death of Kenneth F. Goodall.

The power of attorney was signed with a blue pen. The letters F and G together are made in one sweeping movement. The pen never leaves the paper.

Here is the FG from the FAX of the signature on the purported Trust dated August 24, 1994. We only have this FAX as Hastings and Bank of America refuse to produce the original.

Here the FG is made with two or possibly three strokes of the pen. Heavy black ink is used as opposed to the light blue ink on the power of attorney. The top horizontal line in the F is made with a right to left stroke in contrast to the left to right stroke on the F in the power of attorney.

According to the Forensic Documents Examiner, this creates the likelihood that the documents were signed by two different people, but no final determination can be made until the originals are produced.

Exhibit V

Declaration by Forensic Document examiner David S. Moore stating that there are significant differences between the known signatures of Kenneth and Rachel Goodall and the signatures on the 1994 Trust such that he cannot determine if the signatures are real or forgeries without seeing the originals.

SAM WARE (State Bar No. 105005)
700 Larkspur Landing Circle, #199
Larkspur, CA 94939

Telephone 415-464-4872

E-mail sam@samware.us

Attorney for Sam Sloan,
administrator of Estate
of K. Michael Goodall

SUPERIOR COURT OF THE STATE OF CALIFORNIA

FOR THE COUNTY OF SAN FRANCISCO

In the Matter of the Goodall Family Trust dated September 12, 1990	Case No. PTR-99-273030 Declaration of David S. Moore Hearing Date: Time: Department: 204

David S. Moore declares:

1. I make this declaration based upon my own personal knowledge unless otherwise stated.

2. I am a Forensic Document Examiner. I have a laboratory located at 9010 Barrhill Way, Fair Oaks, California 95628. This laboratory

contains highly sophisticated devices such as microscopes that enable me to determine if a document is authentic or not.

3. I have more than thirty years of document and investigative experience, including assignments with the Crime Laboratories of the United States Army, the United States Postal Inspection Service, the Las Vegas Metropolitan Police, and the California Department of Justice. I have received extensive training regarding handwriting identification, ink and document analysis, and examination, reflected in courses from the United States Army, the United States Secret Service, the Federal Bureau of Investigation, the American Academy of Forensic Sciences, and the California Criminalistics Institute. I have been certified as a "Diplomate" of the American Board of Forensic Document Examiners since 1978. From 1999 to 2002, I served as one of the Directors on that Board. I have published numerous articles in the field of forensic document examination in the Journal of Forensic Sciences, including "The Electrostatic Detection Apparatus (ESDA) and its Effect on Latent Prints on Paper", March 1988; "The Importance of Shading Habits in Handwriting Identification: A Case Study", January 1983; the "Evaluation of a Method to Detect the Site of Rubber Erasures by Powder", October 1981. In addition, I have presented numerous papers at meetings and conferences of the American Academy of Forensic Sciences, the American Society of Questioned Document Examiners, the International Association of

Identification, the Southwestern Association of Forensic Document Examiners, and the Southeastern Association of Forensic Scientists.

4. I have presented numerous classes on questioned document subjects to federal, state and local law enforcement officials, both government and private attorneys, as well as to bank and insurance personnel.

5. I have testified as an expert in the field of questioned documents in justice, municipal, and superior, federal and military courts and administrative hearings in excess of 700 times in more than 20 states throughout the United States, including California.

6. In order to conduct a proper forensic document examination of the original questioned wills and trusts in this instant case, it is my professional opinion that the following tests may be necessary:

a. Visual examination;

b. Microscopic examination;

c. Photographic examination;

d. Ink examination;

e. Handwriting examination;

f. Indentation examination; and

g. Any other non-destructive examination necessary to determine the authenticity of the questioned document.

7. These types of examinations are necessary to evaluate the genuineness of questioned documents. An ink examination allows me to analyze the inks used in the documents and draw conclusions about the use of different inks and to detect whether alternations and/or interlineations have been made. Indentation examination permits me to draw conclusions about whether certain documents were together when they were originally created and also to ascertain whether there is other information contained on the documents in the form of indentations that may provide insight into when the document was created and under what conditions. The other examinations requested may enable me to draw conclusions about the time frame in which the document was created and about the genuineness of the document.

8. The indentation examination, the ink examination, the fluorescence and luminescence examinations require the use of laboratory equipment. For example, the microscope that I use is a stereoscopic trinocular microscope that is not readily portable. The video spectral comparator (VSC) that I use for ink evaluation is not readily portable. The Electrostatic Detection Apparatus (ESDA) that I use for detecting and visualizing indentions is not readily portable. Furthermore, it is often imperative to strictly

control lighting conditions during an examination; this can be done in a laboratory setting, but often cannot be done elsewhere.

9. The various examinations that I have listed and the equipment that I employ during the examination of the questioned documents are routine in cases of this nature. Failure to examine the questioned document in a laboratory setting, with proper instrumentation, may result in loss of valuable evidence that would directly address the issue of the document's authenticity.

10. On May 7, 2012, I conducted a Forensic Document Examination of the wills of Kenneth F. Goodall and Rachel A. Goodall on file at the Marin County Civil Court located at The Civic Center, Hall of Justice, Room 113, San Rafael CA 94901. In this forensic document examination I was assisted by Irene Mariani, Supervisor in the Civil Department of the Clerk's Office. These wills are on file at the Marin County Superior Court. Kenneth Goodall's will is number W001916 and Rachel Goodall's will is number W001919.

11. I have examined at my office laboratory in Fair Oaks, California a white file folder with a business card of James R. Hastings, Attorney at Law, annexed. This white file folder contains the following documents:

Bill from J. R. Hastings dated July 27, 1994

Bill from J. R. Hastings dated July 20, 1994

Business Card of James R. Hastings

Letter by J. R. Hastings to Kenneth and Rachel Goodall dated July 26, 1994

Assignment of Personal Property from Kenneth and Rachel Goodall to the Goodall Trust undated and unsigned marked COPY

Letter from J. R. Hastings to Christine Clausen of Bank of America dated July 26, 1994 informing B of A that it has been named alternate executor of the Goodall Trust unsigned by Hastings and Kenneth and Rachel Goodall marked COPY

Unsigned Declaration of the Goodall Trust, 37 numbered pages plus one unnumbered page entitled SCHEDULE OF COMMUNITY PROPERTY ASSETS

One Page AMENDMENT TO GOODALL TRUST Preamble unsigned and undated marked COPY with one page unsigned Notary Public acknowledgment by James R. Hastings (This two page document is NOT included in the 1994 Trust as submitted by Bank of America but is stapled on top of the unsigned 1994 trust)

Last Will of Rachel Goodall unsigned

DURABLE POWER OF ATTORNEY FOR MANAGEMENT OR PROPERTY AND PERSONAL AFFAIRS unsigned and marked COPY

DURABLE POWER OF ATTORNEY FOR HEALTH CARE unsigned and marked COPY

DURABLE POWER OF ATTORNEY FOR MANAGEMENT OR PROPERTY AND PERSONAL AFFAIRS signed original signed by Rachel Goodall accepted by Kenneth Goodall notarized by James R. Hastings on August 24, 1994 in legal blue backing

DURABLE POWER OF ATTORNEY FOR HEALTH CARE signed original by Rachel A. Goodall dated August 24, 1994 witnessed and signed by James R. Hastings and Nancy Rodgers in legal blue backing

A separate document entitled "Employment of J. R. Hastings Law Corporation Estate of Kenneth F. Goodall" dated

September 19, 1994 signed by James R. Hastings and Endorsed by Rachel Goodall on SEP 27, 1994

12. I have examined documents contained in a Green Ring Binder that appear to be original documents. The Green Ring Binder includes tab markers. It contains the following signed original documents under these respective tab numbers:

Tab 7: Original Letter from James R. Hastings to Kenneth F. and Rachel Goodall dated September 12, 1990, with original signature by James R. Hastings and pencil notes by Kenneth F. Goodall

Tab 9: Durable Power of Attorney signed by Kenneth F. Goodall dated August 26, 1989 and notarized by James R. Hastings

Tab 10: Contributions of Anatomical Gift dated May 16, 1989 and April 26, 1989, signed by Kenneth F. Goodall witnessed by James R. Hastings

Tab 10: Contributions of Anatomical Gift dated May 16, 1989 signed by Rachel A. Goodall witnessed by James R. Hastings.

(This is one of the two original signatures we have of Rachel A. Goodall.)

Tab 11: California Natural Death Act Directive to Physicians dated April 26, 1989 signed by Kenneth F. Goodall witnessed by James R. Hastings

Tab 11: California Natural Death Act Directive to Physicians dated April 26, 1989 signed by Rachel A. Goodall witnessed by James R. Hastings

Tab 11: California Natural Death Act Directive to Physicians dated May 16, 1989 signed by Kenneth F. Goodall, no witnesses.

Tab 12: Durable Power of Attorney on official form signed by Kenneth F. Goodall no date

Tab 14: Personal Affairs Workbook signed on the first page by Kenneth F. Goodall with numerous hand written notes in pencil.

13. I have also examined the following documents which are copies, not originals:

A document entitled "The Goodall Trust" and dated September 12, 1990.

A document entitled "Declaration of the Goodall Trust" and dated August 24, 1994.

A document entitled "Second Amendment to Goodall Trust" and dated January 19, 1999.

14. The conclusions I have reached as a result of these examinations are as follows:

There are no inconsistencies in the signatures of Nancy Rodgers. They were all signed quickly and legibly.

The signatures of Rachel Goodall and Kenneth F. Goodall on the DURABLE POWER OF ATTORNEY FOR MANAGEMENT OR PROPERTY AND PERSONAL AFFAIRS were signed with two different blue pens. This is not inconsistent with the view that Kenneth F. Goodall was hospitalized at the time and that he and his wife Rachel Goodall signed this document at different times and places. I have concluded that these signatures are genuine.

The document entitled AMENDMENT TO THE GOODALL TRUST as filed in San Francisco Probate Court is a copy of a FAX. The FAX markings show it was transmitted on November 24, 2008 at 12:31 PM. The facsimile process greatly distorts the information being transmitted. This distortion is readily evident when attempting to evaluate the authenticity of faxed signatures. From the submitted fax copy, no determination can be made regarding whether the purported signatures of Mr. and Mrs. Goodall were naturally and freely written or whether they contain evidence that would support the belief that they were not genuine. Needless to say in a FAXed document, no determination can be made regarding whether similar or different inks were used to create the questioned signatures. Furthermore, no determination can be made from this fax copy regarding any indentation evidence that may exist, or whether differences exist in paper, staple holes, creases and folds, machine printing, etc. Any and all of these aspects should be considered in evaluating the authenticity of the document - but they cannot because of the poor quality of this faxed document. This is a perfect example of the acronym "GIGO" (Garbage in - Garbage Out). For these reasons, I will need to examine the original document to determine if these are valid signatures. Presently, I am neutral on the question of whether these are authentic signatures. With respect to these questioned signatures, none of the following alternatives can be excluded:

- They may be tracings.
- They may be simulations.
- They may be the product of a "cut and paste".
- They may be genuine.

I declare under penalty of perjury under the laws of the state of California that the foregoing is true and correct.

Executed at Fair Oaks, California this 23rd day of May, 2012.

David S. Moore

Exhibit W

Declaration by Susan D. Scribner for Bank of America as Trustee in Opposition to petition Re Determination of the Particular Action does not constitute a contest dated February 2, 2000.

James R. Hastings, Esq., State Bar No. 079066
J.R. Hastings Law Corporation
18 San Anselmo Avenue
San Anselmo, CA 94960
Telephone: (415) 459-6635
Facsimile: (415) 459-6756

Attorney for Petitioner

FILED
SAN FRANCISCO COUNTY
2000 FEB -2 PM 11:41
CLERK
BY: DEPUTY CLERK

SUPERIOR COURT OF THE STATE OF CALIFORNIA

COUNTY OF SAN FRANCISCO

In Re

The Goodall Trust

NO. 273030

DECLARATION OF SUSAN D. SCRIBNER FOR BANK OF AMERICA, AS TRUSTEE, IN OPPOSITION TO PETITION RE DETERMINATION OF THE PARTICULAR ACTION BY BENEFICIARY DOES NOT CONSTITUTE A CONTEST

DATE: February 9, 2000
TIME: 9:00 A.M.
DEPT: Probate
ROOM: 204

The Bank of America is the Trustee of the Goodall Trust and all Trusts incorporated in the Goodall Trust.

On or about September 12, 1990, Kenneth F. Goodall and Rachel A. Goodall, as Settlors and initial Trustees, established the Goodall Trust through a declaration of The Goodall Trust. At the time of establishment, the Trust was a revocable, intervivos Trust.

Subsequently, on August 24, 1994, Kenneth F. Goodall and Rachel A. Goodall as Settlors and Trustees of the Goodall

Trust executed an Amendment to Goodall Trust. This Amendment was authorized by Section 3.3 of Article 3 of the original declaration of The Goodall Trust and reads as follows:

> 3.3. Power of Amendment While Both Trustors Are Living. During the trustors' joint lifetimes, the trust may be amended, in whole or in part, by both trustors acting jointly.

On August 24, 1994, Kenneth F. Goodall and Rachel A. Goodall, as Settlors and as Trustees executed and Amendment to Goodall Trust. The entirety of the original Declaration was amended to read as an attached Goodall Trust dated the same date.

Kenneth F. Goodall died on September 10, 1994. Subsequently, pursuant to the terms of the Goodall Trust, the Bypass Trust of the Goodall Trust was established and funded with appropriate monies so as to preserve Kenneth F. Goodall's exemption equivalent.

Following the death of Kenneth F. Goodall a Trust Officer of the Bank of America met with Rachel A. Goodall several times and communicated with her by telephone and in writing. Please see the attached letters and notes from 1994 and 1995, which are incorporated in this Declaration by reference.

At this death the most current Will of Kenneth F. Goodall was a Will dated August 24, 1994.

///

The Declaration of the Goodall Trust dated August 24, 1994, directed that Successor Trustees should be determined as follows:

> 7.1 Remaining Trustor-Trustee Serves Alone. Upon the death of the deceased spouse, or if before that time either trustor resigns as trustee, is removed pursuant to judicial procedure, becomes incompetent (as defined in Article Nine), or for any reason fails or ceases to act as trustee, the remaining trustor-trustee shall serve as sole trustee.
>
> 7.2 Successor Trustee. On the death of the remaining settlor-trustee, or if, for any reason, the remaining settlor-trustee ceases to act as trustee, BANK OF AMERICA, NT&SA, San Francisco, California, or any corporation that is a successor thereto by merger, consolidation, transfer of assets, or other manner provided by law, shall be successor trustee.

The Declaration of the Goodall Trust dated August 24, 1994 addressed contests to the Trust as follows:

> 8.3 No-Contest Clause. If any beneficiary under this instrument, singularly or in combination with any other person or person, directly or indirectly contests this instrument, any amendment to this

> instrument, or the wills of the settlors in whole or in part, or opposes, objects to, or seeks to invalidate any of the provisions of this instrument or the wills of the settlors, or seeks to succeed to any part of the estate of the settlors other than in the manner specified in this instrument or in the wills of the settlors, then the right of that person to take any interest given to him or her by this instrument or any amendment to this instrument shall be void, and any gift or other interest in the trust property to which the beneficiary would otherwise have been entitled shall pass as if he or she had predeceased the settlor without issue.

Both the Will of Kenneth F. Goodall, and the Will of Rachel A. Goodall dated August 24, 1994 directed that the Executors be as follows:

> 3.1 Nomination of Executors. I nominate my wife as executor of this will. If, for any reason, my wife fails to qualify or ceases to act as executor, I nominate BANK OF AMERICA, NT&SA, San Francisco, California, or any corporation that is a successor thereto by merger, consolidation, transfer

///

> of assets, or other manner provided by law, as executor of this will.

Both the Will of Kenneth F. Goodall and the Will of Rachel A. Goodall dated August 24, 1994 addressed contests to the Wills as follows:

> 4.5 No Contest Clause. If any person, directly or indirectly, contests the validity of this will in whole or in part, or opposes, objects to, or seeks to invalidate any of its provisions, or seeks to succeed to any part of my estate otherwise than in the manner specified in this will, any gift or other interest given to that person under this will shall be revoked and shall be disposed of as if he or she had predeceased me without issue.

On or about January 19, 1999 the surviving Trustee, Rachel A. Goodall executed a Second Amendment to Goodall Trust. This Second Amendment accomplished three things of import for this proceeding:

First, the Second Amendment, by amending the first paragraph of Section 7.1. of Article 7, confirmed the selection of Successor Trustees for the Bypass Trust as that stated in the Declaration of Goodall Trust dated August 24, 1994.

///

That paragraph reads as follows:

> 7.1 <u>Remaining Settlor-Trustee Serves Alone</u>. On the death of the deceased settlor, or if, for any reason, before that time either settlor ceases to act as trustee, no successor cotrustee shall be appointed to act with regards to the Bypass Trust. Rather, the remaining settlor trustee named in Article One shall have full power to act as trustee of the Bypass Trust and to complete the trust administration.

Second, the second paragraph of the Second Amendment amended Section 7.1 of Article 7 in that it allowed the Petitioner, Kenneth Michael Goodall to act as Co-Trustee to the Survivors Trust (only) during the life of the surviving Settlor, Rachel A. Goodall. In accepting this office, Kenneth Michael Goodall agreed to be bound by the terms of the Trust. The second paragraph of the Amended 7.1. of Article 7 reads as follows:

> After the death of the deceased settlor, at the discretion of the surviving settlor, KENNETH MICHAEL GOODALL, may be appointed to act as cotrustee with regards to the Survivors Trust. This appointment shall be confirmed by KENNETH MICHAEL GOODALL signing a document, such as an Amendment to

Declaration of Trust, in which he agrees to be bound by the terms of the trust.

Finally, Rachel A. Goodall confirmed and ratified "the terms of the Trust as stated in that certain Declaration dated September 12, 1990, as amended August 24, 1994..." Therefore, she reaffirmed and ratified paragraphs 7.2. of Article 7 directing that Bank of America, NT&SA, be the Successor Trustee at her death and she reaffirmed and ratified Section 8.3. of Article 8 directing that there be no contest to this Trust document.

Rachel A. Goodall died on June 7, 1999. At this death the most current Will of Rachel A. Goodall was the Will dated August 24, 1994, the Will in which Bank of America, NT&SA, is to be Executor and in which contests are expressly prohibited.

Accordingly, Bank of America, NT&SA, Trustee, because of the intent stated by the Settlors, Kenneth F. Goodall and Rachel A. Goodall, in all their dispositive documents and because of the apparent intent of Rachel A. Goodall through her communication with the Trust Officer of the Bank of America (see above), (1) opposes any attempt to rewrite the Goodall Trust so as to insert a Trustee at the whim of the Petitioner and (2) asks the court to confirm such action is a contest to the trust.

///

I declare under penalty of perjury that the foregoing is true and correct under the laws of the State of California.

Dated: 2/2/00

By ______________________
SUSAN D. SCRIBNER for Bank of America, as Trustee

Exhibit X

Points and Authorities by James R. Hastings, Attorney for Bank of America, in Opposition to petition Re Determination of the Particular Action does not constitute a contest dated February 2, 2000.

James R. Hastings, Esq., State Bar No. 079066
J.R. Hastings Law Corporation
18 San Anselmo Avenue
San Anselmo, CA 94960
Telephone: (415) 459-6635
Facsimile: (415) 459-6756

Attorney for Petitioner

FILED
SAN FRANCISCO COUNTY
SUPERIOR COURT
2000 FEB -2 PM 11:41
CLERK
BY: DEPUTY CLERK

SUPERIOR COURT OF THE STATE OF CALIFORNIA

COUNTY OF SAN FRANCISCO

In Re The Goodall Trust	NO. 273030 POINTS AND AUTHORITIES IN OPPOSITION TO PETITION RE DETERMINATION OF THE PARTICULAR ACTION BY BENEFICIARY DOES NOT CONSTITUTE A CONTEST DATE: February 9, 2000 TIME: 9:00 A.M. DEPT: Probate ROOM: 204

NO CONTEST CLAUSES ARE STRICTLY CONSTRUED

The California Probate Code describes a "Contest" as "an attack in a proceeding on an instrument or a provision in an instrument." (CA. Prob. C. §21300). The code goes on to state that "No Contest Clause" "means a provision in an otherwise valid instrument that, if enforced, would penalize a beneficiary if the beneficiary brings a contest." (Id). Although subject to exceptions of Probate Code §21306, none of which are applicable in the instance of the Petition before the court, a "No Contest Clause is enforceable against a beneficiary who brings a contest within the terms of the No Contest Clause." (CA. Prob. C. §21303)

AN ACTION REPLACING THE TRUSTEE IS A CONTEST.

Please see the Declaration of Susan D. Scribner for Bank of America, as Trustee, in Opposition to Petition Re Determination of The Particular Action by Beneficiary Does Not Constitute a Contest.

In four separate documents before the court, as outlined in the Declaration and as lodged with the court, the Settlors, Trustees, and Successor Trustee, not only unequivocally named the Bank of America, NT&SA, as Successor Trustee, but stated and reiterated a No Contest Clause over and over again. Further, according to the Declaration, Rachel A. Goodall, after the death of Kenneth F. Goodall, had a preexisting relationship with the Bank of America and later reaffirmed Bank of America as successor trustee.

In the *Estate of Ferber [(1998) 66 Cal. App. 4th 244, 77 Cal. Rptr. 2d 774]* a beneficiary, among other attacks, attempted to remove an Executor who had been named in the document and in the face of an explicit No Contest Clause. After reiterating the facts, the first thing the court stated in this case was: "No Contest Clauses are valid in California and are favored by public policies of discouraging litigation and giving effect to the purposes expressed by the Testator." The court went on to say "because a No Contest Clause results

///

in a forfeiture, however, a court is required to strictly construe it and may not extend it beyond what was plainly the Testator's intent."

Fortunately, for the Beneficiary in this case before the court, the statutes of California allow a "first look" at whether or not an action is a contest, thus avoiding the necessity of any forfeiture. The court in *Ferber* found that "(an) action to remove(an)executor would contravene the express terms of the . . . no contest clause if (the Beneficiary) were unsuccessful." (Id.) The same is true in this instance. An action to remove Bank of America, NT&SA, as Trustee would certainly contravene the express terms of the no contest clause if the Beneficiary were unsuccessful.

Accordingly, I respectively request the court to state clearly to the Petitioner that the action suggested by the Beneficiary does constitute a contest for which forfeiture will follow should he be unsuccessful.

Respectfully Submitted:

Dated: 2/2/00

J. R. HASTINGS LAW CORPORATION

By________________________
James R. Hastings

Exhibit Y

Proof of Service of Points and Authorities in Opposition to petition Re Determination of the Particular Action does not constitute a contest and Declaration by Susan D. Scribner for Bank of America as Trustee in Opposition to petition Re Determination of the Particular Action does not constitute a contest.

PROOF OF SERVICE

I, **KIMBERLEY BYARS**, declare that I am employed in the City of San Anselmo, County of Marin, California; am over the age of eighteen years and not a party to the within entitled action. My business address is 18 San Rafael Avenue, San Anselmo, CA 94960.

On February 2, 2000, I served, in the manner indicated below, the attached:

POINTS AND AUTHORITIES IN OPPOSITION TO PETTION RE DETERMINATION OF THE PARTICULAR ACTION BY BENEFICIARY DOES NOT CONSTITUTE A CONTEST

DECLARATION OF SUSAN D. SCRIBNER FOR BANK OF AMERICA, AS TRUSTEE, IN OPPOSITION TO PETITION RE DETERMINATION OF THE PARTICULAR ACTION BY BENEFICIARY DOES NOT CONSTITUTE A CONTES

along with this Proof of Service on the interested parties in his action as follows:

_XX_____ BY REGULAR MAIL) I caused such envelope(s) with postage thereon fully prepaid to be placed in the U.S. mail at San Anselmo, California to:

SEE ATTACHED LIST

________ BY PERSONAL DELIVERY) I caused delivery by hand to:

________ BY OVERNIGHT DELIVERY) I caused delivery by overnight courier/delivery/U.S. Postal Service.

________ BY FACSIMILE) I caused the document to be transmitted by facsimile and have retained the transmission report.

I declare under penalty of perjury under the laws of the State of California that the foregoing is true and correct, and that this declaration was executed on February 2, 2000 at San Anselmo, California.

Kimberley Byars

KIMBERLEY BYARS

PROOF OF SERVICE

Mr. Kenneth Michael Goodall
461 Peachstone Terrace
San Rafael, CA 94903-1327

Warren Edward Bentley
714 Red Oak
Lewisville, TX 75067

Robert Bedford Bentley
3719 North Hartford
Oklahoma City, OK 73112

Helen Beth Perry
7926 Praver Drive, West
Jacksonville, FL 32217-4156

William Kirk Bentley
1702 East Tenth Street
Shawnee, OK 74801

Julia Geraldine Lemons
2240 Plymouth Road, Apt. 213
Minnetonka, MN 55305-2349

Guide Dogs for the Blind
350 Los Ranchitos
P.O. Box 151200
San Rafael, CA 94915-1200

Ms. Susan Scribner, Trust Officer
Bank of America
Investment Management and Trust Services
P.O. Box 3700, Unit 6753
San Francisco, CA 94137-0001

Robert J. Rothman, Esq.
601 California Street, Suite 800
San Francisco, CA 94108

Exhibit Z

Blank signature pages of the unsigned 1994 purported trust

ARTICLE NINE

SIGNATURE AND EXECUTION

9.1. Execution. We certify that we have read the foregoing declaration of trust and that it correctly states the terms and conditions under which the trust estate is to be held, administered, and distributed. As trustees of the trusts created by this declaration of trust, we approve this declaration of trust in all particulars, and agree to be bound by its terms and conditions. As settlors of the trusts created by this declaration of trust, we approve this declaration of trust in all particulars, and agree to be bound by its terms and conditions. Executed on ______________________ at San Rafael, California.

SETTLORS-TRUSTEES

____
KENNETH F. GOODALL

____
RACHEL A. GOODALL

ACKNOWLEDGMENT

STATE OF CALIFORNIA)
) ss
COUNTY OF MARIN)

On ________________, before me, James R. Hastings, notary public, personally appeared KENNETH F. GOODALL and RACHEL A. GOODALL, personally known to me (or proved to me on the basis of satisfactory evidence) to be the persons whose names are subscribed to the within instrument, and acknowledged to me that they executed the same in their authorized capacities, and that by their signatures on the instrument the persons, or the entity upon behalf of which the persons acted, executed the instrument.

WITNESS my hand and official seal.

Signature ______________________________ (SEAL)

SCHEDULE OF COMMUNITY PROPERTY ASSETS

1. Ten dollars ($10.00); and

2. The real property commonly known as 461 Peachstone Terrace, San Rafael, California.

Exhibit AA

Declaration by Nancy Rodgers, a neighbor and best friend of Rachel Goodall, stating that what purports to be her signature as a witness to the wills is not her signature and she never signed any such wills, although she did sign a health care directive for Rachel Goodall (stating not to use artificial means to prolong life).

SAM WARE (State Bar No. 105005)
700 Larkspur Landing Circle, #199
Larkspur, CA 94939

Telephone 415-464-4872

E-mail sam@samware.us

Attorney for Sam Sloan,
administrator of Estate
of K. Michael Goodall

FILED
Superior Court of California
County of San Francisco
FEB 0 6 2012
CLERK OF THE COURT
BY: [signature]
Deputy Clerk

SUPERIOR COURT OF THE STATE OF CALIFORNIA

FOR THE COUNTY OF SAN FRANCISCO

In the Matter of the Goodall Family Trust dated September 12, 1990	Case No. PTR-99-273030 Declaration of Nancy Rodgers Hearing Date: February 8, 2012 Time: Department: 204

BY FAX

Nancy Rodgers declares:

1. I make this declaration based upon my own personal knowledge unless otherwise stated.

2. I reside at 470 Peachstone Terrace, San Rafael, CA 94903 and have resided there since before 1970.

3. I have examined the signature page of the purported Will of Kenneth F. Goodall, attached hereto in Exhibit A, and the signature page of the purported Last Will of Rachel A Goodall, attached hereto in Exhibit B.

4. At page 7 of each of these Exhibits, I see what purports to be my signature as a witness to those wills, along with James R Hastings as the other witness, purportedly executed on August 24, 1994 in San Rafael California.

5. Although the signatures there looks like mine, I do not recall ever acting as a witness to any will for either Kenneth Goodall or Rachel Goodall at any time, and I am sure that I would remember having done so, so these are not my signatures.

6. I do recall that at some time after Kenneth Goodall died that Rachel Goodall asked me and Barbara Dagitz, another of our neighbors, to be the two witnesses to a legal document pertaining to Rachel Goodall, which I recall being a health care directive or similar document, but never any will at any time.

7. I do not recall ever witnessing any signing of any document by Kenneth Goodall at any time, though I do remember quite clearly my husband and I visiting him in his home shortly before his death.

I declare under penalty of perjury under the laws of the state of California that the foregoing is true and correct.

Date: February 3, 2012 Nancy Rodgers

AFFIDAVIT OF SERVICE

I hereby state that I am not a party, I am over 18 years of age and on July 11, 2013 I served a copy of this Petition for a Writ of Certiorari by mail to the following:

Gary D. Rothstein
Manatt, Phelps & Phillips, LLP
One Embarcadero Center, 30th Floor
San Francisco CA 94111

Alicia A. Adornato
Attorney for Guide Dogs for the Blind
Reed Smith LLP
101 Second Street, Suite 1800
San Francisco CA 94105

Guide Dogs for the Blind
Mr. Thomas Horton
Planned Potential Beneficiary Giving Director
Guide Dogs for the Blind, Inc.
350 Los Ranchitos Road
San Rafael, CA 94903

Sam Ware
700 Larkspur Landing Circle, #199
Larkspur, CA 94939

John L. McDonnell, Jr.
Reed Smith LLP
1999 Harrison Street, 24th Floor
Oakland CA 94612

Don A. Lesser
1010 B Street
Suite 350
San Rafael CA 94901

Jerry R. Hauser
Miller Hauser Law Group
4 Embarcadero Center, 39th Floor
San Francisco, CA 94111

James R. Hastings
1003 3rd Street
San Rafael, CA 94901

Robert J. Rothman
601 California St Suite 1600
San Francisco, CA 94108

Deborah Rodgers
Bradley Luxury Division
851 Irwin Street
San Rafael CA 94901

Roy Hoppe
461 Peachstone Terrace
San Rafael CA 94903

Frank Thornally
461 Peachstone Terrace
San Rafael CA 94903

Julia Bentley Lemons
Apt. 308
12800 Marion Lane W
Minnetonka, MN 55305-1368
Surviving Sibling of Rachel Goodall

Robert B. Bentley
Timberwood Senior Living Rm. #34
5020 WE 44th St.
Oklahoma City, OK 73135

Helen Beth Bentley Perry
7926 Praver Drive W
Jacksonville,FL 32217
Surviving Sibling of Rachel Goodall

Clenda Fern Bentley Zinar
4536 Chatman Street
The Colony, TX 75056

Beverly Gale Bentley Young
2316 Trenton
McKinney, TX 75070

Vickie Bentley Hankins
14580 NE 6th
Choctaw, OK 73020

Jeffrey Bentley
4701 N Douglas Boulevard
Spencer, OK 73084

Chad Everett Bentley
1609 Teepee Trail
Kingsland, TX 78639

Jeanette Goodall Phillips
152 S llth Street
Salina, Kansas 67401

Kristin Kane
University of California
Berkeley College of Engineering
College Relations
208 Mclaughlin Hall #1722
Berkeley, CA 9472A-1722

Bank of America
1000 4th St.
San Rafael, CA 94901

July 11, 2013

Made in United States
North Haven, CT
06 November 2026

21817312R00157